D0205524

Ask Yourself:

ARE YOU WILLING TO TAKE CHARGE
OF YOUR LIFE?

If your answer is yes, then you are holding the simple, revolutionary solution in your hands. *GAINING CONTROL* takes you step by step through Robert F. Bennett's fail-proof Control Method. You'll examine your "belief window"—the principles that color and influence everything you do. And you'll discover how to read other people's belief windows—and understand, even predict, their actions. You'll find out how to use the Control Model to evaluate your beliefs, understand which are harmful, and use those that are helpful to enhance your life and empower you.

GAINING CONTROL will help you to:
- deal more successfully with problems—even those that seem beyond your control
- gain the crucial insights you need to make better personal and business decisions
- improve difficult relationships by identifying behavior principles and patterns
- succeed, grow and reap the ultimate reward of control—*freedom*

DO IT NOW!

With a background in both government and industry, Robert F. Bennett is president and chief executive officer of The Franklin Institute, Inc., consultant to many of America's leading corporations and public organizations. In addition, Mr. Bennett is a popular speaker, seminar leader, and consultant on the principles contained in *GAINING CONTROL*.

Most Pocket Books are available at special quantity discounts for bulk purchases for sales promotions, premiums or fund raising. Special books or book excerpts can also be created to fit specific needs.

For details write the office of the Vice President of Special Markets, Pocket Books, 1230 Avenue of the Americas, New York, New York 10020.

GAINING CONTROL

Your Key to Freedom and Success

ROBERT F. BENNETT
With Kurt Hanks & Gerreld L. Pulsipher

POCKET BOOKS

New York   London   Toronto   Sydney   Tokyo

*To my father, who has the clearest window
of anyone I know.*

POCKET BOOKS, a division of Simon & Schuster Inc.
1230 Avenue of the Americas, New York, NY 10020

Copyright © 1987 by The Franklin Institute, Inc.

All rights reserved, including the right to reproduce
this book or portions thereof in any form whatsoever.
For information address Franklin Institute,
8436 West Third Street, Los Angeles, CA 90048

ISBN: 0-671-67632-6

First Pocket Books trade paperback printing October 1989

10 9 8 7 6 5 4 3 2 1

POCKET and colophon are trademarks of
Simon & Schuster Inc.

Printed in the U.S.A.

Contents

About This Book

Let me share three stories with you.

First, here's a recent experience I had with the concepts you'll meet in this book:

Everyone Wants to Be In Control

The office of the U.S. attorney in Utah has embarked on an ambitious education program on drug abuse, aimed at the high schools. Brent Ward, the U.S. attorney for Utah, contacted The Franklin Institute, Inc., to see if we could help him help the students deal with issues of self-esteem, because he felt that lack of self-esteem was one of the reasons kids turn to drugs. The result of those conversations was an agreement on my part to address assemblies in every high school in the state of Utah, along with representatives from Brent's office.

Most of these talks have gone very well. The usual pattern has been for us to talk to the entire student body. In one circumstance, however, the principal of the high school put me in a different situation with all the makings for an ugly experience.

The situation had all the makings of an ugly experience.

Instead of bringing in all the students, he selected about fifty kids that he considered as hard-core druggies and alcoholics and put only them in the room. I got a taste of what things would be like as I watched a member of the U.S. attorney's office outline the law on drug dealing in a way that he hoped would make the kids think twice before becoming involved. It's a presentation that's usually quite sobering.

Not this time. The kids first laughed at him and then started to challenge him. They knew as much or more about the law than he did. "You can't touch us," they said. "We're under eighteen." They quoted chapter and verse with respect to the rights of minors, and practically hooted him off the stage.

I sat there thinking, "This is really going to be grim." I realized that all the material I normally used wouldn't work at all with these kids.

I sat there thinking, "This is really going to be grim." I realized that the material I normally used wouldn't work at all. When I stood up, I reached back into my army days and, drawing on the vocabulary of that experience, said to the kids, "I go around the country speaking for a living, and I've gotten pretty good at reading audience reaction. From your reaction this morning, I can tell that you think all of this is (expletive deleted)."

"Yeah, man!" They all cheered. "It is (expletive deleted)!"

I then tried challenging some of them directly, and one kid in particular. I won't repeat the exchange, but the end result was that he stamped out of the room, cursing me. It was not a good beginning.

I then described to them the concept of the Control Model, which you will meet in this book. I set up five chairs in the front of the room, each one representing one aspect of the Control Model. I put one student in each of the five chairs, and started walking the kids through the concept of the Control Model. They were still hostile, but I managed to hold the group together. I asked them to identify their perceptions and actions, which we then pushed through the Control Model. At each stage of the process I would have the boy or girl sitting on the appropriate chair be the one to explain how that section of the model applied to the question at hand.

The atmosphere started to change from hostility to mild interest, then to involvement. When we got to the end of the hour, I felt that I had reached them and said, "Well, we're out of time. I hope you understand what I've been trying to say."

"More!" they said. "We've got to have more of this. Can't we come back?"

I looked at the principal. "I can come back after lunch," I said. "Is it all right if we spend a little more time on this?" The principal said, "Sure."

After lunch the kids came in—eager this time. The kids who had sat on the five chairs in front went straight to their chairs so that nobody else could take their places. Now the reactions were intense, with the kids heavily involved. I picked out one in particular, and asked him why he drank—what basic need was he trying to fill in his life?

"I'm not trying to fill any need," he sneered. "I drink because it's fun."

"All right," I said. "How much do you drink?"

"I drink eight or ten beers a week, and then I get drunk on the weekends," he said.

"Okay," I said. "You believe drinking is fun. Let's look at your belief window and see what else you have written on it. Do you think you're ever going to be an alcoholic?"

"No way, man. You think I'm gonna be an alcoholic with just a few beers a week and then a drunk on the weekends? No way."

"Okay, let's look at that." I started putting that through the Control Model, in an effort to find out whether the perceptions he believed were accurate or not. (The Control Model does this in a nonjudgmental way.) The rest of the kids started calling out, "Hey, man, he's an alcoholic right now!"

You can't understand the full flavor of what was happening until you've read the book. Just keep in

> **As we worked with the Control Model, the atmosphere started to change from hostility to mild interest, and then to involvement.**

> **Here was a businessman in his forties, with short hair, white shirt, and a dark suit, in a room with fifty scruffy teenage druggies and alcoholics, teaching abstinence—and getting away with it.**

> One boy said, "I've been arrested, I've been in jail, and I've been worked with by parents, teachers, and all kinds of do-gooders. This is the first thing that's been offered to me that made any sense."

mind this scene—a businessman in his forties with short hair, white shirt, and a dark suit in a room with over fifty long-haired, scruffily dressed teenage druggies and alcoholics, teaching abstinence and getting away with it. As you read and learn more about the Control Model, that mental picture will help you understand its power.

When I finally finished, one of the kids came up to me and summarized the whole experience in terms of his own life. "I've been in counseling for seven years," he said. "I've been using drugs and alcohol for longer than that. I've been arrested, I've been in jail, and I've been worked with by parents, teachers, and all kinds of do-gooders. This is the first thing that's been offered to me that's ever made any sense."

The concepts in this book work.

Where These Concepts Originated

Where did they come from? That's the second story. In 1984, a group of us formed The Franklin Institute, Inc., to teach time management seminars and sell a datebook organizer we call the Franklin Day Planner. We soon realized that we needed some management help. I called Bob Bennett, an old friend who was then president of Microsonics Corporation in Los Angeles, and asked if he would be willing to fly up to Salt Lake City to meet with us. To cut through the details, he liked what he saw enough to leave Los Angeles and come on board as Franklin's president and chief executive officer.

Not long after that, we reached out for assistance to make sure that our seminar curriculum was the best that could be put together, and that it met the needs of our market. We contracted with two communication "gurus" (at least that's what we called them), Kurt Hanks and Jerry Pulsipher, to help us do that job.

Kurt and Jerry did that, but they also helped us realize that what we were really dealing with were the issues of productivity, rather than just the mechanics of time management. They decided to research the issues of productivity to see if there might not be a book in it, which The Franklin Institute, Inc., could publish. We agreed that it was worth a try.

After working on it for a while, they came in and said to Bob, "The more we dig into this, the more we realize that what we're really dealing with is not 'productivity' but 'control.'"

Bob asked what you may have asked, when you saw this book's title: "What do you mean by *control?*"

"The whole issue of how people seek to control their lives—their careers, their relationships, their work situation, and their reactions to the things that happen to them. People who gain control automatically become productive."

Before long, Bob started to be missing from the office for a morning here or an afternoon there, because he was off with Kurt and Jerry talking about "belief windows" and something they called the "Control Model." Frankly, some of the other executives in the company worried a little about the amount of attention he was giving to this project, because we were still very small and needed his hand firmly on the administrative tiller. However, since he was the CEO, no one really wanted to cross swords with him on the issue, and he continued to work with Kurt and Jerry on the book.

We all seek to control our lives: our careers, our relationships, our reactions to events and situations. People who gain control automatically become productive.

Then something else started to happen that none of us really noticed at first. The concepts taught in the book began to show up in the day-to-day management of the company. Bit by bit, Bob would teach the rest of us the relevant business applications of the belief window and the Control Model. Our corporate meetings began to use the vocabulary of these ideas. Without realizing it, we turned ourselves into a laboratory in which these concepts were tried and proven. We used the Control Model to examine our own decision-making process, to

Without realizing it, we turned the company into a laboratory in which these concepts about control were tried and proven.

assess our competition and our customers, to guide our internal personnel and strategic decisions, and to check and make corrections on our overall goals. Looking back on it, we realize that the control model has been a significant contributor to our growth which, since the time the present company was put together, has been more than tenfold in terms of employees and twentyfold in terms of sales. (As of publication date, we're teaching over 3,000 people a month, in some of America's biggest companies—Dow Chemical, General Motors, Merrill Lynch, Rockwell International, and the like.)

As a result of the process of using these concepts in his own business assignment, Bob truly became the book's principal author, so it's a different book, with a different author, from what it started out to be.

About Bob Bennett

Now I'll tell you the third story—Bob's story. Some readers may already be familiar with his name because, for a period of time about fifteen years ago, he was in the public eye as a suspected "player" in the Watergate drama. One of the reasons he has reacted so strongly to these concepts is because they resonate with his own passage through the crucible of that time.

Bob's degree is in political science. In 1963 he went to Washington as press secretary to Congressman Sherman P. Lloyd, and then did a brief stint as administrative assistant to his father, Senator Wallace F. Bennett.

In 1964 the J.C. Penney Company opened a Washington office and asked Bob to head it; at age thirty, he was the youngest representative of a major corporation operating in the nation's capital. He established himself as enough of an expert on dealing with Congress that, when Richard Nixon was elected president in 1968, Bob joined the administration as a head of the congressional liaison operation at the Department of Transportation. His performance was so outstanding that Secretary John A. Volpe picked him out of more than 100,000 employees to receive the department's highest civilian honor.

When he left the administration two years later, he purchased the Robert R. Mullen Company, a well-established and highly reputable Washington-based public relations and management consulting firm. He immediately started bringing in additional clients, including the Howard Hughes organization. For a young man still in his thirties, his future seemed bright indeed. But there was a hidden bomb in all this.

One of the employees of the Mullen Company at the time Bob bought it was a former C.I.A. officer named E. Howard Hunt. In 1971 Bob received a phone call from Charles Colson at the Nixon White House, asking if Bob would be willing to allow Hunt to serve as a consultant to the president on a part-time basis. (Bob says he wishes he had *that* call on tape; he remembers Colson saying to him, "I don't think Howard's White House duties will interfere too much with his work for you, Bob. He can do his work for us mainly at night and on weekends.")

After his early successes in Washington D.C., Bob's future seemed bright indeed. But a hidden bomb was ticking.

Then came the Watergate break-in. When Howard Hunt was first implicated in it and then formally charged, both the Mullen Company and Bob became the subjects of intense investigation, official as well as media. Instead of servicing the needs of his clients, Bob spent hours and days answering questions. He testified before grand juries, U.S. attorneys, and congressional investigating committees. He was given a completely clean bill of health after all of this was over, but enough of an aura of possible involvement clung to him and the firm that his previously uninterrupted string of career successes was over. People who had sought out his advice and counsel became conveniently unavailable when he wanted to talk with them; many of his phone calls to former colleagues went unreturned. His clients began to disappear.

One who stayed with him was the Howard Hughes organization, but they wanted his services full-time. Bob moved his family to California in 1974 and took up duties as director of public relations for Summa Corporation. He began to rebuild his career, not as a political consultant, but as a manager.

Then Howard Hughes died "without telling anyone where he put the will," as Bob puts it. Everything at Summa changed, and Bob was faced with a choice of either leaving the company or moving to Las Vegas to take up a career in the gambling business. He chose to leave Summa and stay in Los Angeles.

He worked for several firms and attracted some outside consulting clients, but they were a lot smaller than the Fortune 500 companies he had served before. He found himself immersed in the problems of small and start-up companies, and came to learn that management challenges at that level were often very different from those that faced the corporate giants.

Throughout a career vastly more varied than most, Bob moved through a crucible of stress, change, and uncertainty that forced him to confront and deal with these issues on a very real level.

In 1980 he was offered the presidency of Microsonics Corporation, a firm that made microrecords and microphonographs. A public corporation with a NASDQ listing for its stock, it was losing in excess of three million dollars a year. Meeting its challenges marked the final stage in Bob's transition from political advisor to consultant to line manager. Microsonics reached breakeven eighteen months after he joined it. As I said, that's where he was when I called to ask him to help us get The Franklin Institute, Inc., off the ground.

You can now see why he emerged as the principal author of this book. Throughout a career vastly more varied than most, Bob moved through a crucible of stress, change, and uncertainty that forced him to confront and deal with these issues on a very real level.

When the high school assembly I mentioned earlier began, I was afraid I was in for one of the more ugly experiences of my life. I reached for the ideas in this book to help me, and when it was over, I felt about nine feet off the ground.

The Control Model works. You have a great experience ahead of you, as you learn about it and see the changes it can produce in your life.

Hyrum W. Smith,
Chairman of the Board,
The Franklin Institute, Inc.

GAINING CONTROL

Our Need for Control

Like many of you, I have read the articles about unemployment and what it does to the psyche of the modern American, but I had never really understood the full impact until I became unemployed myself.

In America today, we equate a person's worth with what he or she is doing. (Almost automatically, we assume a medical doctor to be intrinsically "better" than a postman.) When we meet someone new, we usually ask, right up front, "And what do you do?" People respond with the labels of their jobs.

That is why the loss of a comforting label can be so devastating, and why we look for other ways of saying it when it happens to us. In my case, I preferred telling people I was "doing a little consulting"—it seemed to soften the stigma of not having a more specific label.

Use of such euphemisms, however helpful they are in social situations, still can't hide that gnawing feeling that occurs in your gut in such circumstances, the feeling that says that you are unemployed because somehow you are just not good enough to hang on to a job. Even though I could tell myself a thousand times that I was where I was as a result of circumstance, I couldn't escape the bite of that particular worm.

An "Aha" Experience

I remember very clearly the moment and the setting when I realized that that idea wasn't true. In my search for clients, I had gone to a meeting with an executive whom I had known casually while in the job I had just left. He was working on a project that seemed interesting, and had asked for my advice. I had put on my best suit, made sure that it was properly pressed and that my shoes were shined, and had gone to talk with him, hoping that he wouldn't mention my embarrassing "lack of label" status.

The loss of an esteem-giving label can be devastating, and we look for ways to save face. In my case, I preferred to tell people that I was "doing a little consulting."

The meeting went well. The problems that he was confronting were problems on which I could comment intelligently. Indeed, the direction in which he chose to move was the one that I recommended, and he promised, sincerely, to "keep in touch." There was some hope that this would turn into a genuine source of income.

As I was driving back home, coming through Topanga Canyon over the Santa Monica mountains, I reviewed the meeting in my mind. Perhaps it was natural that my thoughts centered primarily on the amount of money that I might be able to charge for my services, should he contact me again. But as I let my mind wander in a wider perspective, I also thought about all the people who had told me, in a thousand subtle ways, that I had "lost" it—that my status was deserved, that I was a failure. Without consciously doing so, I had started to believe them. The anxiety I had felt in going to the meeting just concluded, my desperate hope that it would be the way to gain back a secure position, confirmed that. I was afraid I *had* lost it, and that all those people were right.

But what I had done at the meeting belied that

notion. It suddenly hit me: I *was* a competent person—whether I had a socially acceptable "label" or not. I had something to offer. I *had* acquired skills in my life. I was, in the language of a popular book of the time, *O.K.*

As I said, I can still remember the moment, and I could drive you now to the place on Topanga Canyon Boulevard where I was when this particular insight hit me. As I look back on it from the perspective of this book, I realize that was the moment that I took control of my job search. While I might not have been able to influence everything around me, I could be (and was) in charge of myself.

That realization, the sense of being in control, was more important than all of the external circumstances that I faced.

We All Need to Feel "In Control"

I told Kurt and Jerry about that moment while we were sitting in a restaurant one night, discussing the basic issues of this book. Frankly, I did it as casual social conversation; I considered it inconsequential. But they insisted that it was not. "Everyone has those kinds of insights," they said. "They are the 'aha's,' the pivotal points in our lives that come without fanfare or fireworks, but still make all the difference." They urged me to write the experience into the book (and told me of similar ones they had had, walking down an office corridor or sitting at a kitchen table at three in the morning), because, they said, "A sense of being in control, at least of oneself, is essential to a healthy and productive outlook."

While we all believed that, and went ahead with the book on that assumption, we didn't have any folders full of research data supporting it. Then we came across the *New York Times* of October 7, 1986, where we read:

> **It suddenly hit me: I was a competent person—whether I had a socially acceptable label or not.**

> **The "aha" experiences we have are pivotal points in our lives. They come without fanfare, but they make all the difference.**

The feeling of being in control, of having a say over what happens in one's life, has far reaching consequences for physical and mental health.

Researchers are finding that *the sense of being in control, and the desire for such control, are more crucial and pervasive aspects of personality than psychologists have previously realized.* Increasing the sense of control among elderly men and women living in convalescent homes made them happier, increased their alertness and—perhaps most dramatically—lowered their mortality rate, over a period of eighteen months, by 50%.

The increased control came from simple changes, such as allowing the convalescent home residents to decide what they would have for meals, when the phone would ring in their rooms and how the furniture would be arranged. (Italics added)

> **A desire to be in charge of our own lives is born in each of us. It is essential to our mental health and success that we take control.**

In short, a desire to be in charge of our own lives, a need for control, is born in each of us. It is essential to our mental health, and our success, that we take control.

What happens to that desire? The article goes on to discuss what happens to too many children.

Some studies have found that, over the course of elementary school, a student's sense of autonomy and innate motivation to learn steadily decreases. "This suggests that an important source of children's energy for learning is being lost," Dr. Ryan said. ". . . the more a student feels controlled from outside the less pleasure he feels from inside. He ends up being turned off to learning."

What I felt in the Santa Monica mountains that day was certainly "pleasure from inside"; I had been blinded to it before because I was seeing life according to the labels of others, rather than the way it really was. I had given control away. It was my false perceptions, not outside circumstances, that were blocking me.

We *Can* Change Incorrect Perceptions

> **The sense of being in control is far more crucial than psychologists have previously realized.**

How do we change perceptions? We usually need help. Consider a procedure followed by certain police stations in Japan. When they get a drunken arrestee, these Japanese policemen tape record the prisoner's behavior while he is "under the influence" and then, when he is sober, require him to sit and listen to himself in the cold light of morning.

The man's own memory tells him that he had been all-around "good company" the night before: uninhibited, witty, and fun loving. The tape-recorded memory proves that he was loud, obnoxious, self-centered, and boring.

Our own memory may tell us that we were all-around "good company" the night before, when in reality we were loud, obnoxious, self-centered, and boring.

Police using this technique report that they get few repeat offenders; their drunken "guests" had never realized how their actual behavior appeared to others. They had never seen or heard an objective representation of the way they acted. They had relied on their own perceptions of things, and those perceptions were false. Until they understood that, they kept on making the same mistake.

Far too many of us are like the detainees in the Japanese police station, seeing things through our own perceptions of reality; I know I was. We may not be alcoholics, but all of us are addicted to something—some self-destructive belief—that is hurting our lives in a practical way as well as stunting our mental and spiritual growth.

Ask yourself the following:

- Are there assignments on your job that never seem to work out properly, which you attribute to circumstances "beyond your control"?

- Do you deal with someone—family member, business associate, personal friend, customer—whose behavior you can never seem to fully understand? Does that frustrate you?

- Do you have a sense of helplessness or powerlessness when confronted by outside forces or groups primarily because you can't see any reason why they act the way they do and therefore can't anticipate their actions?

- Are you living with other major frustrations in your life, that are made even more frustrating by the fact that all of your efforts to get on top of them seem to fall short of the goal?

An incorrect, self-destructive belief may be hurting our lives in a physical way as well as stunting our mental and spiritual growth.

Affirmative answers to any of the questions listed are symptomatic of a lack of *understanding* of what is really going on, which then makes it difficult, if not impossible, to know whether one can *influence* the direction things will take or must accept and *adapt* to the inevitable. The dilemma is summarized in "The Alcoholic's Prayer:"

Lord, grant me the serenity to accept the things I cannot change,

The courage to change the things I can,

And the wisdom to know the difference.

People who have achieved fulfillment in their lives are those who are in control—of themselves, their careers, and the relationships and conditions around them.

People for whom that prayer is fully answered—who can have the three things listed—are people who are in control of themselves, their careers, and the relationships and conditions around them. They have achieved a fulfillment in their lives that the rest of us might envy. As you reread the prayer, realize that it is all about choices and making decisions.

The *central thesis* of this book is that your life is the sum result of all the choices you make, both consciously and unconsciously. If you can control the process of choosing, therefore, you can take control of all aspects of your life, and overcome the frustrations inherent in the questions listed above. You can find the freedom that comes from being in charge of yourself.

The *purpose* of this book is to explore the choosing process, to help you understand how it works, and then arm you with a tool, like the tape recorder in the police station, that will enable you to see the consequences of your choices through a prism other than that provided by your own perception.

That's all there is to it, really. The book is short, making the basic points and asking some questions, but leaving it up to you to apply the lessons in the context of your own life. There are a lot of examples, but the best ones for you will be the examples you identify out of the wellspring of your own experience, like my own while driving down Topanga Canyon Boulevard and thinking about being unemployed.

The Belief Window

Out in front of every person in the world is a large window through which he or she views everything that goes on. Although it is invisible to the naked eye, it is very real. Not only do we see the world through it (looking out), but we also use it as a filter through which all of the world's data is passed (coming in). If there is data that we do not wish to receive, we use our window as a shield to keep it away from us.

The belief window is firmly fastened to the person's head.

Each belief window is unique to the individual.

On the preceding page is a visual representation of this process at work. The individual depicted has "bought" a particular principle (believes the principle to be true) with respect to the capacities of men and women, and he is in the process of writing that principle on his window, where it will influence everything he does as a manager (or husband) from now on.

We live our lives by the principles we have written upon our belief windows.

All of us have chosen to write on our individual windows the set of principles by which we live. These principles can be lofty, rooted in deep moral and spiritual concepts; they can also be petty, springing from our own set of jealousies and prejudices.

Let me give you some examples. The Catholic nun known as Mother Teresa has a different set of principles written on her belief window than most of the people who live with her in India. When she looks out at the world, her belief window tells her that every individual, regardless of the caste or social status into which he or she was born, is a child of God, worthy of love and attention. As a result, she spends her life serving the "untouchables" in Indian society, those whom others instinctively avoid.

In contrast, consider the view through the windows of the individuals who created the Ku Klux Klan in the Southern States in America after the Civil War. As these folks looked out on the world, the principles on their windows told them unequivocally that blacks were inherently inferior to whites and should be "kept in their place." They proceeded to establish a reign of terror among whole sections of their communities: burning crosses, preventing blacks from voting, and, when they thought it necessary, engaging in lynch-mob justice.

Most of us are neither Mother Teresas nor klansmen, but the process applies to us as well. Once we have adopted a principle and written it on our window, it determines the course of our behavior.

Whenever anything relating to that particular principle should arise, we act according to the principle and reject any data that says we should be doing something else.

Thus the man shown in Kurt's illustration will dismiss any examples of excellence on the part of women managers, branding them as "atypical." On the other hand, anecdotes that prove the superiority of men will be embraced as "I told you so's." These will further reinforce his commitment to the principle that he sees as he looks through his window at performance in the workplace, and will "prove" that he is right, at least to him.

Belief windows can be collective as well as individual; people who share the same principles come together in groups, which helps sustain the group.

Belief windows can be collective as well as individual.

People who share a common belief window look, act, and think alike.

Insiders

Outsider

Companies have belief windows; their effects are sometimes called "corporate values" or "distinctive management styles." Since leaving the J.C. Penney Company I have paid attention to retailing trends, and I can see clearly that the view through the window at K-Mart is different than the one in front of the management at Nordstrom's.

For a lesson in differing perceptions of the same set of facts on an even grander scale, listen to the speeches at the next Democratic convention, describing America's position in the world, and then do the same thing when the Republicans are on the air.

The belief window is neither "good" nor "bad"—it is simply there.

A belief window can be very helpful, if the concepts written on it are correct. Once you have adopted the principle that the world is round, for example, your window will not allow you to take seriously the arguments of the Flat Earth Society. This will save you a lot of time and trouble if you are an engineer working at NASA.

So, the belief window is neither "good" nor "bad"—it is simply there. The better you can see what is written on an individual's belief window, the more you can predict his future responses, explain his past actions, and motivate needed changes, because:

> **Human beings, either individually or acting in groups, cannot behave in a way that is inconsistent with their belief windows.**

That being so,

> **The first step toward taking control of your life is taking a good look at what's on your window, and *accepting the possibility that some of the things on it are wrong*.**

Let me illustrate with case studies of some real windows.

1. The Girl Who Believed She Was Ugly

In the various group presentations I have made of these concepts, I have often used, as a sample principle that most of those present may have bought at one time or another, the following:

"Suppose," I say, "that somewhere, sometime, someone you trusted told you that you were ugly. (Haven't we all been told that at some time in our lives?) Suppose you bought that principle and put it on your window. If it never came off again, after mature reflection, it could affect the rest of your life."

I said this to one group in which sat a particularly attractive girl, one you would notice when she walked into the room. The only problem with this girl's looks was that she never seemed to smile; she *really* didn't smile at this point. She also didn't participate in any of the discussion that followed.

Afterward, her boyfriend came up to me and wanted to talk. He told me, incredibly, that this girl was convinced that she *was* ugly. He said her mother had told her that often when she was a little girl.

"I can't get her to accept the idea that she is attractive," he said. "It is a major part of her self-esteem problems, and it is affecting our relationship."

Of course it affected their relationship. When he told her he thought she was attractive, her window told her, "He's either lying to you or else he's too stupid to realize how ugly you really are." Neither trait was one that she would want to have in a boyfriend.

By accepting *her mother's principle* about her looks and putting it on her window, this young woman had given her mother control over this aspect of her life; she could not take control herself until she replaced her mother's principle with one of her own.

> By accepting her mother's evaluation about how she looked, this young woman had given her mother control over her life.

If this young woman can accept the possibility that the principles on her window might be false and examine them accordingly, she will probably discover that she is in fact attractive not only to her young man but to others as well, and that he is not lying to her when he tells her that. She can then take control of her feelings toward him, instead of allowing her mother to dominate the situation from the grave.

Questions for you, from "The Girl Who Believed She Was Ugly"

(If seeing answers to these questions is hard for you, try talking them out with someone else— usually someone else's view of your window is clearer than your own.)

• *What statements about your self-image do you have on your window?*

• *Where did they come from?*

• *How might they be challenged?*

• *Are you getting contradictory signals from others, which your window is preventing you from seeing?*

• *Is there someone in your life—a parent, former boss or teacher, former lover—who, even without thinking about you, is in control of your behavior in certain situations?*

---

2. The MBAs Who Had the Answers

At one point in my career I was consulting with a company that was having its troubles, with the chief executive officer under considerable pressure from the board to produce; changes were being demanded, fast.

This CEO did not have a formal business education, having risen through the ranks on the basis of his excellent performance in lesser jobs. Somewhere along the line he had bought and put on his window this principle: *Formal education is the ul-*

timate mark of achievement. Only those who have its credentials are fully capable. Do you see what acceptance of that principle would do to his self-confidence level, in the time of stress?

He could not quit his job and go for an MBA himself; help had to come from the outside, from the nation's business schools. (Naturally, he ignored suggestions from people already in the corporation.) Deciding that Harvard was the best of the best, he brought some freshly minted Harvard MBAs into the company as his personal advisors— an action that was consistent with the view through his window. Everything would now be well.

As these young men showed up, it was hard for the rest of us in the company not to be impressed with them. They were uniformly bright, obviously well trained, and asking all the right questions. However, when they started implementing their programs to "save" the company, it was clearly an outline for disaster.

A number of us huddled together at the lunch tables in the executive dining room and puzzled as to how such bright young men could be doing such incredibly stupid things. We asked each other, "What do they teach them at the Harvard Business School?"

We wondered how such bright young men could be doing such incredibly stupid things.

In the midst of this I was called by Jim Beggs, later the administrator of NASA. At the time he was executive vice president at General Dynamics; we had worked together at the Department of Transportation, where he had been the undersecretary. Passing through town, he suggested that we have dinner together. He is himself a Harvard MBA, so, after bringing him up to date on the company and its problems, I put the question directly to him: What do they teach you at the Harvard Business School?

He asked how extensive the young men's authority was. When I told him that it was virtually company wide, he said, "That's the first mistake. You must never give a Harvard MBA any line authority for at least two years."

That didn't answer my question. Why not? What were they taught at the Harvard Business School that made them incapable of handling power?

It goes in as "question everything." But in the minds of the inexperienced, it comes out as "trust no one."

"Understand, Bob," he said, "that if they remember nothing else—if they are taught nothing else—they come out of Harvard with this one concept firmly implanted in their minds: Question everything."

I thought about that for a moment and said, "I can't challenge that—it's a sound intellectual posture."

"You don't understand," he said. "It goes in as 'question everything.' But in the minds of the inexperienced, it comes out as 'trust no one.' When these young men sat across the desk from you and asked you what your problems and insights were, they weren't listening to your answers. They were saying to themselves, 'Either this guy is stupid or he is lying.' They learned nothing from you or anyone else.

They will finally learn that they have to start trusting people even while questioning established procedures.

"In about two years, it will finally dawn on them that they will have to start trusting other people if they are going to be effective, even while questioning established procedures. Never give them any line authority until they learn that lesson."

Question everything. That's a principle these young Harvard graduates were taught at school, and it is a sound one. However, when it went on their windows as "trust no one," it distorted the view accordingly, and they lost control of the situation. (They should have questioned themselves, along with "everything.")

However bright and well trained they may have been, none of them were with that company a year after their graduation, nor was the chief executive who had hired them.

Questions for you, from "The MBAs Who Had the Answers"

- *Have you bought the principle that credentials are more important than content? (Are there any people with whom you have dealt whose advice was bad, but to whom you listened simply because they "should" have known what they were talking about?)*

- *Do you work (or live) with someone who could teach you something, but whose comments you habitually ignore?*

- *Have you ever rejected a sound suggestion simply because you hadn't thought of it first?*

---

3. The Puppet and the Puppeteer

Several years ago, a friend of mine, whom I'll call Joe, had an "aha" experience—one of these times where he actually saw his window and how it was controlling his emotions. The experience centered around his father.

Joe's father was a domineering man who wanted to mold Joe in his own image and force him to follow the same career path and hold the same values and view of life. From the time Joe was a teenager, he rebelled, deliberately moving in different directions. As soon as he could, he left home to get away from his dad, hoping that his resentment against the father's interference would finally go away. But it didn't; indeed, it grew as the years passed. The young man never felt "free" of his father's attempts to control him, and ached to do something about it.

Joe finally decided to "let it all hang out," to have things out with his father once and for all. He knew the old man was strong-willed, and that the confrontation would be a nasty affair for his mother, with whom he had strong ties and a loving relationship. But he felt that he had to get it off his chest, regardless of the consequences. It would be "good" for him, psychologically, according to his window.

> He never felt "free" of his father's attempts to control him, and he ached to do something about it.

During the drive to the small rural community where his parents lived, Joe thought it all through again and realized something for the first time: He had been acting like a puppet for all these years, responding to his father's pull on the strings. The "aha" was the realization that *he* (Joe) *was the one who had kept the strings tied to the puppeteer.*

He saw that the strings connecting him like a puppet to his father were the principles he had written on his window with respect to his father; when he had accepted as truth those principles that sprang from his father's behavior, he had unwittingly opened the door for his father to control him, even when his father was not present.

There were three ways he could react to his dad. One, he could rebel, which was what he had been doing all these years. That meant that, as a puppet, he would do just the opposite of what the puppeteer commanded (a typical response for many teenagers). If Dad says to be in at ten o'clock, I'll stay out until midnight, just to show him.

But all such rebellious behavior is really doing is changing the hand and foot strings around, so that when the puppeteer moves the hand string, the foot responds; the puppeteer is still controlling. The boy didn't stay out until midnight because he wanted to, but *because of what Dad said.* The string was still attached.

Rebellion doesn't cut the strings; it simply repositions them.

Well, he thought, perhaps I can become the puppeteer. Many teenagers think, "I'll slip from Dad's control by controlling him," and they do just that. They know just what to do to make their parents furious—which profanities to use, what rock music to play, which friends to bring home, what clothes to wear, and so on. They end up in control by becoming the puppeteer.

But a puppeteer is always dependent on his puppet for his act to work; the strings still go from one to the other. Neither is free. If my friend's happi-

The "aha" was the realization that he was the one who had kept the strings tied to the puppeteer. When he came to the realization that *he* controlled how he would react to his father, the strings fell away of their own accord.

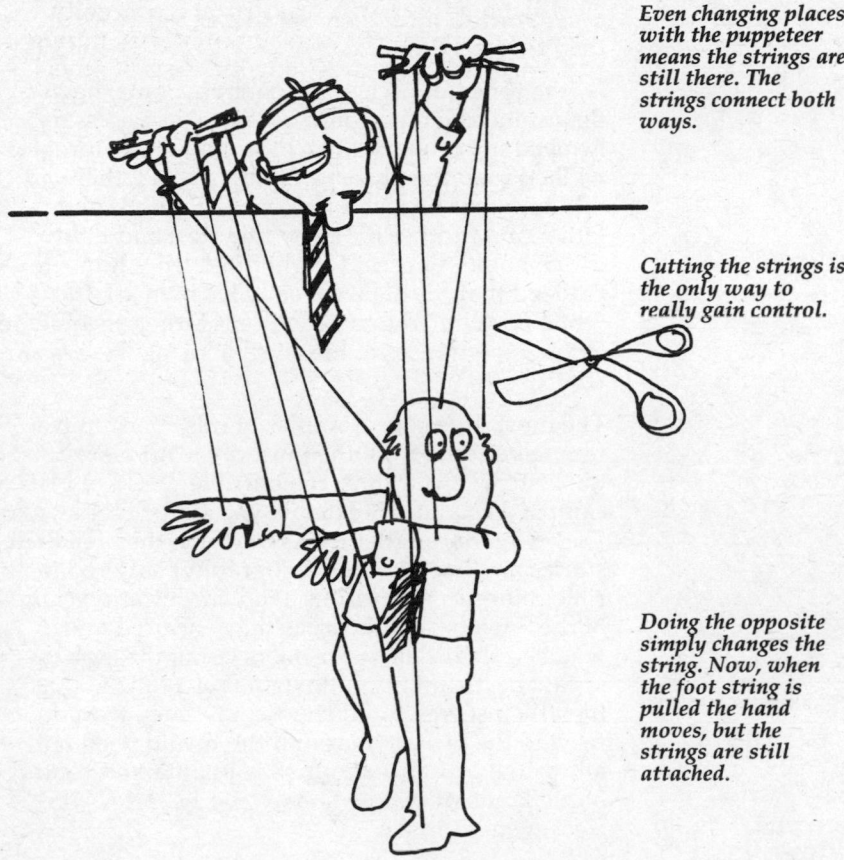

Even changing places with the puppeteer means the strings are still there. The strings connect both ways.

Cutting the strings is the only way to really gain control.

Doing the opposite simply changes the string. Now, when the foot string is pulled the hand moves, but the strings are still attached.

ness in the relationship was dependent on his ability to manipulate his father, he would stay, ultimately, in his father's control.

Becoming the puppeteer was not the answer.

Then, he saw that he could simply cut the strings. Why? Because they were dependent on what was written on his window, which he could control, rather than what was on his father's, which he could not. There was no point in shouting at his dad; the solution lay with himself. The minute he came to the realization that *he controlled how he would react* to his father, the strings fell away of their own accord.

By the time he reached his parents' home, he had determined that no confrontation was necessary; he need not let his father control him anymore. He walked in to the house, went up to his father and told him that he loved him, visited with both his father and mother for a few minutes, and then drove home—a great weight lifted from him. He realized that his life was really his own affair; while he still had to deal with his father, it could be through responses of his own choosing. He was in control.

The most dramatic examples of this concept in action have come from the most dreadful places in the history of our time, the horrible world of prison camps. Alexander Solzhenitsyn, Viktor Frankl, and Corrie ten Boom (the books in which they tell their stories are listed in the bibliography) suffered terrible things in the prisons and concentration camps of the Soviets and Nazis, as they endured and watched their fellow prisoners going through unspeakable torments. But when they realized that they themselves could choose how they would react to the brutality around them, and need not allow it to brutalize them, they maintained control of the kinds of people they would be. They were free, even in prison.

Questions for you, from "The Puppet and the Puppeteer"

- *Are there strings attached to you that you could cut; is there someone in your life to whom you always overreact? (This could be a boss, "uppity" subordinate, sassy teenager--even a TV commentator whose views you hate.)*

- *Are you playing puppeteer with anyone?*

- *What would happen if you cut these strings, and just got on with your life?*

What's on Your Window?

It's time to look at your own window.

Following is a list of topics. Go down it and ask yourself, "Which of these do I buy and which do I reject as incorrect?"

The way you react to each statement will give you an indication of what's on your own belief window; if you don't completely accept the statements as they stand, you may want to make some notes or comments in each area, to clarify what you think.

Let's begin with the public issues:

ABORTION:

- *An unborn child is a person.*
- *A woman has the right to choose what happens inside her own body.*

THE ARMS RACE:

- *The Russians want to take over the world by force.*
- *The Russians have reason to be frightened by America's arms buildup.*

EDUCATION:

- *Schools should go back to the basics.*
- *Schools are too traditional.*

COMPARABLE WORTH:

- *People should be paid on the basis of what their jobs are intrinsically worth, regardless of the law of supply and demand.*
- *It is impossible to set wages fairly except by market forces.*

HOMOSEXUAL RIGHTS:

- *One's sexual orientation is innate and cannot be changed; homosexuality is like having green eyes.*
- *Homosexuality is learned behavior.*

AND, FINALLY:

- *There is a conspiracy of _____ (fill in the blank) that is controlling everything.*

Now, on a more personal basis:

SEXUAL RELATIONSHIPS:

- *Men hate women.*
- *Sexual ability is tied to physical appearance.*
- *Sex is a normal and necessary physical function, like breathing.*
- *Sex involves moral decisions.*

RELIGION:

- *God is a _____ (Catholic, Jew, Protestant, etc.)*
- *God will save only those who confess Jesus Christ as Savior.*
- *God doesn't care what you believe as long as you are a good person.*
- *There is no God.*

MUSIC:

- *Rock music is Satanic.*
- *Rock music is loud, but morally harmless.*
- *Rock music is physically harmful.*
- *Rock music is NOT music.*

FAMILY RELATIONSHIPS:

- *Mom and Dad will always love me, regardless of what I do.*
- *My parents, or husband, or wife will never understand me.*
- *My parents, or husband, or wife made me the way I am.*

SELF-ESTEEM:

- *My worth as a person is determined by:*
    - ☐ *The praise I receive from other people*
    - ☐ *The things I own (clothes, cars, houses, etc.)*
    - ☐ *The importance of the job I hold*
    - ☐ *The way I look*
    - ☐ *Whom I marry (or date)*
    - ☐ *How often I win at games*
    - ☐ *Any combination of the above.*

RESPONSIBILITY:

- *I'm a pawn of outside forces, and can't do anything about it; it's not my fault.*
- *Everything that goes wrong is my fault.*

And, finally:

- *Anyone who disagrees with me is stupid.*

This list is by no means intended to be exhaustive; it is offered simply in an effort to get you to recognize that there may be alternatives to the principles that you have bought. Go back over it again, review the notes, if any, that you made, and ask yourself, in each instance, "Could I perhaps be wrong about this?"

Summary

Each of us (or each group of us) sees the world through a window on which we have written the principles we believe to be true. Where those principles are true, the view through our window is clear; where they are false, the view is misleading. So:

> **YOU *can* be in control of your life, depending on the truth of the principles by which you choose to live it.**

Put that on your window, right up front.

Okay, I hear you saying, all well and good. But what exactly do you mean by "the principles written on the window"? Aren't principles basic truths that can't be challenged, things that don't change? Define your terms.

The next section deals with that.

PRINCIPLES:
The Great Canadian Gray Goose
Flying Machine Company

Bob Mullen, the founder of the Washington-based P.R. firm I purchased in the early 1970s, began his career as a reporter. One of his early papers was in Denver. On his lunch hour there one day, with nothing much on his mind, he was walking through a section of town that was unfamiliar to him when he saw, on a storefront, a sign proclaiming "The Great Canadian Gray Goose Flying Machine Company." He was intrigued by the name and decided to step inside to see if there might be a story in it.

The store was empty of the usual store furniture; instead of counters and displays, it had rows of chairs set up in classroom style. At the front of the store, facing the chairs, was a small podium. Other than the sign with the company name, there was no evidence that this was a place of business. Several people were sitting in the chairs, obviously waiting for something to happen.

Bob asked what was going on and was told, "It starts in a few minutes." Now he was truly curious and sat down to wait. More people came in.

In a few minutes a middle-aged man whom we will call Fred walked into the store and up to the podium. He was pleasant-looking and friendly to all, and, after greeting them warmly, began talking.

He was the president of The Great Canadian Gray Goose Flying Machine Company, he said, and he was there to tell them about the company and its product. To understand both, they must first understand the premise on which the company was built, namely, that God is the Greatest Engineer of All.

If God is the Greatest Engineer of All, Fred said, then it stands to reason that God's creations will be better engineered than man's. That being the case, if we wish to build an airplane (or flying machine, if you will) we should follow God's pattern in our planning. This Fred had done, using as his model the finest of all of God's flyers—the Great Canadian Gray Goose. If we wish to build the very best flying machine we possibly can, Fred maintained, then it must be as much like this bird as it is humanly possible to make it.

> If we wish to build the best possible flying machine, Fred maintained, then it must be as much like the Great Canadian Gray Goose as it is possible to make it.

Fred had studied the Great Canadian Gray Goose carefully and had discovered the secret of its extraordinary flying ability. "When the wings are raised (and here, according to Bob, the man spread out his arms and raised them, with the fingers wide apart) the feathers are turned and spread, like my fingers, so that the air can pass through. The wings rise without hindrance through the air. On the downward beat, however (here he closed his fingers, making a flat hand as he moved his arms down), the feathers turn to close off all passage of air, so that the wing can beat a powerful, lifting stroke.

"Open when rising, closed when pushing down, open when rising, closed when pushing down, that's the secret—the secret of the Great Canadian Gray Goose. I am going to build a flying machine that is based on that secret."

All of this was delivered with the utmost good cheer and sincerity, and Bob found himself liking the man a great deal, in spite of his amusement over the idea. Then came the sales pitch.

"I want you to help me," Fred said. "I need money to make this machine a reality. To get it, I am willing to sell shares in the company. I want you to buy those shares, and help me build a flying machine based on the principles of the Greatest Aeronautical Engineer of All.

"I realize that it is a risk—all investments are. I don't want to have you take a risk that will hurt you if things don't go right. I don't want your life savings. All I ask is that you buy one share each, for ten dollars. Indeed, I won't let you buy any more than that, because you might not be able to afford it and I wouldn't want that on my conscience. But if you can afford ten dollars, I will take that and you will all be my partners in a noble enterprise that will grow to the glory of God and earn you money at the same time."

And with that he passed the plate, up and down the aisles. A number of people gave him ten dollars.

When the store had cleared of people, with the president of The Great Canadian Gray Goose Flying Machine Company standing at the door and personally greeting each one, Bob remained and spoke to him at some length. Fred was a former minister who had come to Denver for his health—in those days, it was known for its clean, crisp air—and hadn't been able to find work; there was no place for a displaced minister to preach and nothing else he could find that he felt he could do. One day, pondering the beauty of the birds and other creations of God, he had hit upon the idea that caused him to form his company. He had chosen this unusual way to raise money, he said, "because it is the only way I know."

Bob went back to the office to write the story, and followed the company's progress after that. He was present at Denver's Stapleton Airport—then

"I want you to help me build a flying machine based on the principles of the Greatest Aeronautical Engineer of All."

newly built—when The Great Canadian Gray Goose Flying Machine, complete with movable wings and little airholes that were open on the upstroke but closed on the down, collapsed while attempting takeoff. And he sadly chronicled Fred's indictment on charges of stock fraud.

What Was on Fred's Belief Window?

If you had approached Fred with the concept of the belief window and asked him to identify the principles that were written on his, I believe that he would have told you the following: "I believe in God. I believe in working hard. I believe in being fair and hurting no one. I believe in full disclosure of my intentions."

He may or may not have added:

"If I hold to these basics, I am sure to win out in the end."

He did not win out in the end; instead, he found himself penniless, humiliated, and charged with serious crime. Which of the principles listed above had led him astray?

Ignorant of the true principles of aerodynamics, Fred could be sincere in his belief in God, and work as hard and honestly as he could, and still fail to get off the ground.

The answer, of course, is none of them, standing alone. However, there were other principles at work that he had ignored.

There were the principles of aerodynamics. Whether you believe in God or evolution as the creator of the Great Canadian Gray Goose, the fact is that the bird flies in accordance with the laws of aerodynamics, virtually none of which Fred knew. It is not the *flapping* of the wings that is crucial— the goose can fly with its wings held motionless— but the airfoil *shape* of the wing (along with many other factors) that matters. Ignorant of all this, Fred could be as sincere as possible in his belief in God, and work as hard and as honestly as he could, and still fail to get off the ground.

While I doubt that any of us is planning to build a flying machine, we all make the same kind of mistakes that Fred made; that is, we commit ourselves to a set of impressive moral principles and then blunder ahead in the belief that these will protect us from the real problems of living. I don't wish to downgrade the importance of moral principles—indeed, I'll speak very highly of them later on—but we need to spend some time looking at them in context, to understand more about the axioms we wittingly or unwittingly etch into our windows.

What Are Principles?

For most of us the word *principle* means a statement of a natural law, or an explanation of things as they really are. As an example, consider again "the principles of aerodynamics," by which we mean those forces in nature that make it possible for an object (or creature) that is heavier than air to fly.

"Basic principles" is a phrase we take to mean "things that cannot be changed."

That being so, we can isolate a principle and then use it as a guide to achieve order or predict results. Mendel, the Swiss monk who tended sweet peas in his garden, thought he detected a basic principle of nature in the way those flowers reproduced themselves. He isolated that basic principle and then went on to develop the overall principles of genetics, by which he could predict (and to an extent control) what would happen to future generations of both plants and animals.

Like a scientist, we can isolate a principle at work in a given situation, and then use it as a guide to achieve order or predict results.

Albert Sloan moved to do the same thing at General Motors—discover correct principles of management, apply them correctly, and thereafter both predict and control the future.

So to the degree that principles are statements of natural laws, they can be a guide to lead us to the discovery of further natural laws.

So far, so good. What gets us in trouble is the fact that we often adopt an idea, and put it on our

In any situation, the mixture of true principles and false ones masquerading in the language of truth can be very confusing.

belief window as a principle, without knowing whether it is in fact an accurate statement of a natural law or just a misconception on our part. Thus, when we look through our windows at the world, we are not really sure whether we are seeing true principles—the laws of aerodynamics—or false ones that appear to be true because they are "in the language of truth."

The mixture between the two can be very confusing. Fred at The Great Canadian Gray Goose Flying Machine Company may well have been working on a true principle when he adopted the value of hard work; his problem came when he worked hard to build a flying machine that was based on false principles of aerodynamics.

Thus, while we may write our principles on our windows one by one, they never stand alone; they are always influenced by the relationship they bear to the other principles that are there. The view through our windows is always a mixture of truth and misconception, and our decisions are influenced by the contexts in which we make them. To illustrate:

A President's Principle

Before becoming president, Dwight D. Eisenhower spent his entire adult life in the military, except for a brief stint as president of Columbia University. Everything that was written on his window came out of that context. As president of the United States, the principles of decision making and leadership that he followed, deeply etched on his window, came instinctively from the totality of his military career. He didn't think about *why* he viewed things as he did—like all of us, he just did.

In 1954, the French, with whom he had worked closely less than ten years before, approached Eisenhower for military aid for their beleaguered garrison at Dien Bien Phu. Many of his advisors urged him to provide it. The principle at stake, they said, was one of opposing communism, wherever it appeared, a principle with which Eisenhower agreed.

However, there was another principle on his window. Sometime during his years of experience in the military he had written this on it: "Don't get bogged down in a land war in Asia." This principle acted *in relationship with* his opposition to communism to provide the context in which his decision with respect to the French request would take place.

If the French had been seeking American air power to help them repel an attack from the Germans, undoubtedly Eisenhower would have furnished it with little second thought, but a land war in Asia was anathema to him; instinctively, he resisted it. While he staunchly supported the anti-communist concept of fighting Ho Chi Minh in Vietnam, what he had on his window from his military context instinctively kept him from committing the levels of troop strengths that came at the hands of his successors.

John Kennedy, Eisenhower's successor, thought Ike unduly timid in foreign policy. JFK wanted to "get the country moving" with "Vigah!" (I remember the T-shirts that said just that, in the early 1960s.) He turned the issue over to his Secretary of Defense, Robert McNamara, who became a primary architect of America's role in Southeast Asia.

McNamara had a different set of instincts than either Eisenhower or Kennedy. As a professor at Harvard Business School, a planning officer in the Pentagon during the Second World War, and finally a member of senior management at Ford during the glory days before Toyota appeared in America, he bought the principle that just about any problem could be reduced to measurable numbers.

When he looked through his window at Vietnam, it told him to gather all the information he could and run it through the computers at the Pentagon. He could then use his own considerable analytical powers to project the result. He did so, and ad-

A strongly held principle from Eisenhower's military experience acted in relationship to his personal opposition to communism to provide the context in which he would make his decision on aiding the French.

vised two presidents that an American military initiative in Vietnam would be productive of American foreign policy goals. Presidents Kennedy and Johnson led us into that land war in Asia which Eisenhower's window insisted would have been a mistake.

> Our process of "buying" principles comes out of the totality of our experiences. As a result, we will inevitably end up with some "principles" that are right, some that are wrong, and some that are shades in between.

Principles and the Scientific Method

Scientists understand the power of that concept. Consider the parallel between the belief window and what has come to be known as "the scientific method." Substitute the word *principle*, as used above, for the scientist's *hypothesis* and see what happens:

In the scientific method, a scientist observes the world around him and attempts to discover a basic truth, a natural law. When he thinks he has one, he states it as if it were true, calling it a "hypothesis." However, even as he states it, he accepts the possibility that it may, in fact, be false, in whole or in part.

By accepting the possibility that some of the principles he was testing might prove to be wrong, Edison vastly increased his chances of eventually being right.

So he tests it, by whatever means are at hand, in as many contexts as he can find. When he has the totality of the experience in front of him—all of the test results—he determines whether his original hypothesis was true or false, with no moral stigma attached to the discovery that the original thought may have been in error.

As Thomas Edison once said to someone who bemoaned his lack of progress in the effort to find filament for the electric light bulb, "No, I'm making a lot of progress. I have discovered hundreds of things that won't work."

By accepting the possibility that some of the principles he was researching might prove to be wrong, Edison vastly increased his chances of eventually being right. What was wrong with Fred and The Great Canadian Gray Goose Flying Machine was not his unquestioning belief in God, but rather his failure to test the aeronautical assumptions that he based on that belief in the crucible of other relationships and contexts.

One can hold a firm belief in God and still build an aircraft that flies.

Reading Principles; Predicting Behavior

The following news story was widely circulated and reprinted in early 1982:

> Moments after Air Florida's Flight 90 left the runway at Washington's National Airport, it was clear that the Boeing 737 was not going to fly. As it shuddered and stalled, the co-pilot said, "We're going down," and the pilot answered grimly, "I know it." With a deafening crash it slammed into the Fourteenth Street Bridge and plunged into the icy waters of the Potomac. Witnesses watched in horror as the fuselage, which had broken free of the tail section, rolled gently and sank beneath the surface, its rows of passengers still strapped into their seats. Only the tail remained afloat—with six people clinging to it.
>
> One of them was Arland D. Williams, Jr., a balding, graying, middle-aged bank examiner and father of two, who was on his way to an investigation in Florida. Although divorced two years previously, he was soon to be remarried and was probably the one with the best chance, for while the others had broken limbs and collapsed lungs, he was relatively free of injury. All he had to do was hang on until help arrived.
>
> At 4:20, nineteen minutes after the crash, the rotors of the U.S. Park Police helicopter were heard thwacking through the cold winter air. Bert Hamilton, who was treading water about ten feet from the floating tail, took

the single lifeline dangling beneath the chopper and passed it under his arms. The others watched while the helicopter carried him a hundred yards to the Virginia shore and returned. This time Arland Williams caught the line. Instead of wrapping it around himself, however, he passed it to flight attendant Kelly Duncan. Soon she too was safe.

On its third trip back to the wreckage, the helicopter trailed two lifelines, for its crew knew that survival in the river was now only a matter of minutes. One of the lines was aimed at Williams. He caught it again and again passed it on, this time to Joe Stiley, the most severely injured survivor. Stiley slipped the line around his waist and grabbed Priscilla Tirado, who, having lost her husband and baby, was in complete hysteria. Patricia Felch took the second line, and the helicopter pulled away. Before it reached the shore, however, Priscilla Tirado lost her grip and fell back into the water, so the helicopter, on its next trip, had to return for her.

Arland Williams' turn came at last. The chopper crew was eager to meet him and salute his selfless heroism. But, as they approached the wreckage, they saw that he was gone. It was 4:30. He had been in the paralyzing cold for twenty-nine minutes—a minute or so too long.

Rescue Officer Gene Windsor wept as he related the incident to his wife. "He could have gone on the first trip," said the pilot, Donald Usher, "but he put everyone else ahead of himself. Everyone."

Why? No one will ever know, of course. Family and friends described the man as quiet, competent, cheerful, humble—average. Reporters combed his background for some clue that would make sense of it all but nothing came to light. Arland Williams remains a mystery to this day.

> **The consistency with which Arland Williams repeated this behavior clearly indicates that he was following a principle that was firmly etched on his belief window.**

His Pattern Was Consistent

Arland Williams is no mystery, because there is a pattern to what he did that day in the icy waters of the Potomac. Each time the rope was dropped, he passed the rope to someone else. The consistency with which he repeated this pattern clearly indicates that he was following a principle that was firmly etched on his window. *Behavior patterns do not happen by accident.*

We cannot be completely certain of what his principle was without having other examples of his behavior. Whether it had root in some specific religious teaching or was simply an expression of a general moral value to which Arland Williams gave great weight, we cannot be sure. We can, however, postulate that some principle involving the importance of selflessness was governing in his life.

Having identified it, we can now predict with some confidence what his behavior would have been in a different context. Suppose Arland Williams were in a fire, for example? What would his past behavior predict that he would do?

Look at the following graphic, in which you see a new element—rules. Rules are nothing more than specific applications of general principles:

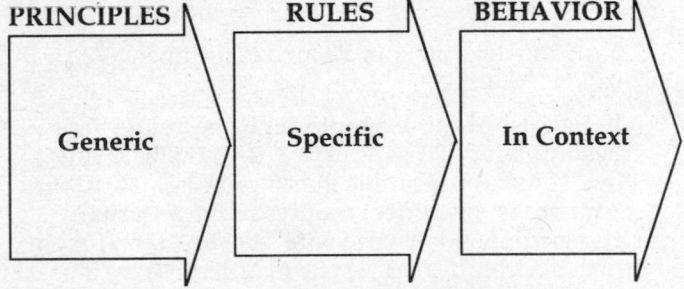

PRINCIPLES — Generic
RULES — Specific
BEHAVIOR — In Context

As we've seen in previous sections, the principles you have bought—right or wrong—are the driving force that leads to behavior. If you know the principle someone else has on his window, you can construct the rule that will apply in a situation and then predict his behavior, moving from left to right.

In the case of Arland Williams, we have reversed that. In terms of the graphic, we have read from behavior back to principle, from right to left. The beauty of the process is it works either way— behavior to principle, principle to behavior—in giving us predictive power.

Let's run some examples, starting with a hypothetical one:

Assume that a man who believes as a matter of principle that a happy marriage is dependent upon the physical attributes of the wife. Write that down inside the "PRINCIPLE" arrow.

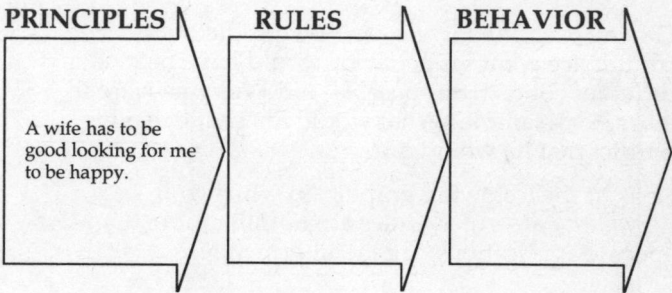

Now move to the middle arrow, the one we've called "RULES."

In the case of this example, let us postulate a beautiful girl—Miss America, if you will. A rule that could apply to this man's principle is: "If Miss America is the perfect beauty, and my marital success depends on my wife's beauty, then I must marry a Miss America type in order to have a happy marriage."

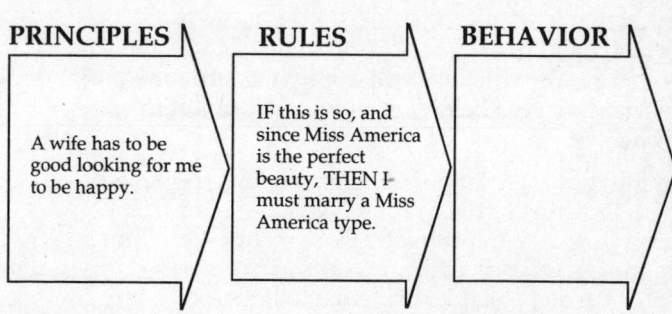

Over in the "BEHAVIOR" arrow, then, we can safely assume that this individual will start to maneuver himself into situations where he can hope to gain an introduction to either a current or an immediately past beauty contest winner, preferably Miss America. By reading from left to right—from principle toward action—we can predict what is going to happen.

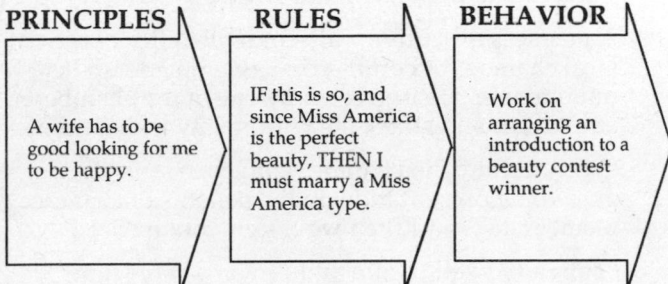

PRINCIPLES

A wife has to be good looking for me to be happy.

RULES

IF this is so, and since Miss America is the perfect beauty, THEN I must marry a Miss America type.

BEHAVIOR

Work on arranging an introduction to a beauty contest winner.

Now read it in reverse. If you find someone who is interested in marriage and is spending all of his free time trying to arrange an introduction to Miss America (or at least the closest thing he can find in his neighborhood), then you can read the chart back from right to left and identify the principle that he is following, even if it has never been explicitly stated.

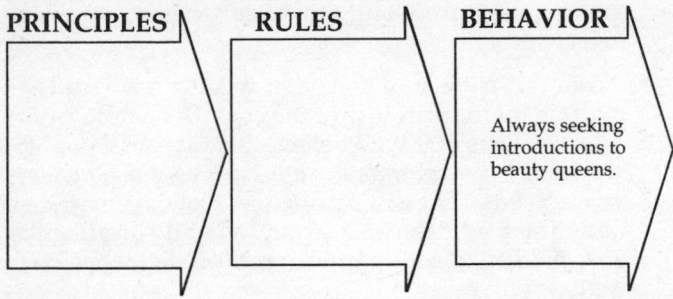

PRINCIPLES

RULES

BEHAVIOR

Always seeking introductions to beauty queens.

What principle is he following?

Because we usually don't know a person well enough to be sure of his or her principles in advance, the normal use of the graphic is to start with the BEHAVIOR section, looking for a pattern, to see if a principle can be extracted from it.

Try it with these real-life examples:

The Rule-bound Employee

A business executive walks into the office of the local chamber of commerce, having made up his mind to join. He is greeted by one of the chamber's employees and states the reason why he has come.

"Wonderful," the chamber employee says. "I'll give you a presentation on the benefits of chamber membership, and then we'll sign you up."

"I already want to join and I'm on a short time fuse. Let me give you my check, and enroll me as a member."

"No, I can't do that," says the chamber employee. "First I have to be sure you understand what you're getting into."

"I only have five minutes. How long will the presentation take?"

"The presentation takes seven minutes."

This was an actual experience. The chamber employee insisted on running through the presentation, time expired, and the executive has yet to join the chamber.

The chamber of commerce employee clearly believed that it was essential to follow the rules regardless of any other considerations or consequence.

From this pattern of behavior, what can we read written on the window of the chamber employee? Clearly, he is one who believes that it is essential to *follow the rules regardless of any other consideration or consequence.* That is his principle. Now, mentally put him in a traffic emergency, a family argument or a political discussion--can you predict what his actions will be?

A Case of Mixed Signals

The following is an exercise through which we have gone at The Franklin Institute, Inc., in an effort to figure out what was going on at another firm. (They're not a direct competitor, but they're close enough that it makes sense for us to keep track of what they're doing.)

Since we didn't know what their management principles were, we started with their actions. Here's the list we drew up.

First, this company recently produced an extremely expensive product. We know from comments made by some of the suppliers that the raw material costs were very high; the company "went first class" in every buying decision. We listed that as one action.

Next, the company's sales material is voluminous, always printed on the finest quality paper, and in full four-color. Being in the publishing business ourselves, we understand exactly what all that costs. It is clear that "no expense has been spared." We listed that as a second action.

Another one of the company's products was a very long time in the making—a great deal of money was spent for outside consultants and advisors.

Is a pattern beginning to emerge?

Top management had seemed to buy the principle that cost control doesn't matter.

Finally we learned that, in an effort to deal with some of their administrative problems, the board of directors of this company had just hired several very high salaried executives. These men came on in addition to the present management team—no one was dismissed in order to make room for them.

At this point we were willing to read the pattern from this series of actions and fill in what we considered to be a guiding principle of the firm. Before going on, see if you can guess what it was.

We decided that the company's top management had bought the principle that *cost control doesn't matter.*

The managers of the firm in question would probably disagree with that, claiming instead that they had adopted a principle attributed to the Japanese—quality above all else. However, the Japanese have proved that quality can be attained while still keeping a close eye on costs, and the managers of this company have not done that. I stand by our analysis; the managers of this firm believe that cost control doesn't matter.

Now, no competent business person would ever consciously embrace such a notion; there must be another principle at work here, interacting with the first. What might it be? Here's a list of additional actions:

- The company has a record of considerable success in selling high ticket items, usually at a substantial markup. Some of this success has come over the dire predictions of observers who insisted that their prices were too high.

- The company has developed an extremely loyal following, with many of its customers almost fanatic in their support of the company's products.

- The company's founders have relatively deep pockets, having experienced considerable success in other ventures.

Does that shed any light on what's on their window?

After evaluating these two principles, we predicted that the company's next product would be high priced and promoted on the firm's reputation rather than its usefulness. We were right on all points.

From this pattern we decided that the principle that overrides (and masks the effects of) the incorrect concept that "cost control doesn't matter" is the idea that *the abilities and reputation of the company and its principals are so great that they can sell anything, at almost any price.*

From the above two principles, we predicted that their next product would be high priced, heavily tied to their previous products, and promoted primarily on the basis of the reputation of the firm producing it rather than its usefulness in the marketplace. When the product showed up in the retail stores, we were right on all three points.

You Understand the Process; Try it Yourself

Get a sheet of paper and reproduce these three arrows. Then follow the instructions:

A: *Pick someone you admire, list his or her actions in (or under) the "Behavior" arrow, and see if you can identify a consistent pattern.*

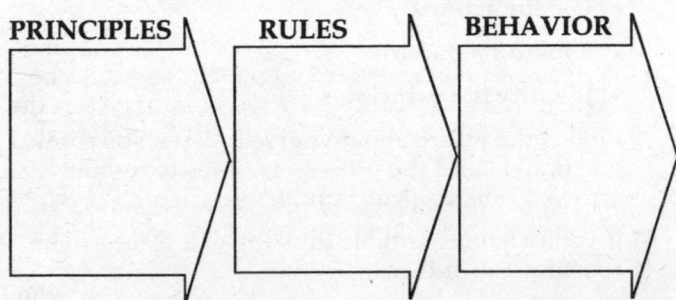

PRINCIPLES   RULES   BEHAVIOR

B: *Next, analyze that pattern to see if you can reconstruct the rules and the principles that are being followed. Write these in the appropriate arrows.*

C: *Remember, when you can accurately identify the principles involved you can safely predict the behavior of that individual in other circumstances.*

Try not to agonize too much over the process; just write out a list of actions and see what happens.

Could you do it? Are you confident of your forecast? Whatever your answers, repeat the process using someone you don't particularly care for. List the actions, look for a pattern, then identify and write down the principles that appear to be behind the pattern. Finally, imagine a future context and predict behavior.

Now try it the other way—take someone you admire whose principles are well known, and see if you can predict the behavior. Imagine a context, apply the known principle in that context, and write out your description of how your subject will act.

When you've finished that exercise, do it again with someone for whom you have no respect.

When you think you understand the process, it's time to use the arrows to analyze *your* problems.

Identify an area in your life or on your job that seems out of control—an area where you're having problems. List your behavior with respect to this problem and see if you can identify a pattern.

Remember, you're going to:

- **List the actions**
- **Look for a pattern**
- **Identify the principles**

Predict the future about yourself. When you think you understand the process, it's time to use the arrows to analyze your problems.

If you're having trouble thinking of a place to start, consider one of these:

- Is it possible that you are manipulating someone under the guise of "helping" them? Take a troublesome relationship and look for a pattern that might indicate that.

- There is destructive behavior on the part of a member of your family. What are your continuing reactions to this behavior?

- There is conflict at work—are your regular actions contributing to it?

- What principles have you bought about the role of money in your life; what are your patterns of spending?

- Are you being fair with your employer, or are your work habits just going through the motions?

You needn't take one of these, of course—this is your choice. When you've picked your topic for analysis, write down your examples of behavior with respect to it and start through the steps. (Try to forget for the moment that you are the one being examined; be as objective as you can.)

The "aha" experience will be the point at which your principle emerges. Your reaction to it may be denial: "I'm not really that kind of person."

However, be honest with yourself, especially at this time. Have you accurately reported your past actions, and is the pattern clear? If so, it is likely that you are that kind of person, good or bad, and the statement you have written is predictive of how you will behave in the future.

Your initial reaction to an "aha" experience may be denial: "I'm not really *that* kind of person."

We found in the first section that we behave consistently with our belief windows. If you have gone through the exercise I have outlined, the principle staring up at you from your paper, extracted from the pattern of your behavior, is what is written on your window. You will behave consistently with it until you decide to change it.

Those individuals and groups that are locked in a pattern of failure can expect that the cycle will repeat itself, regardless of the context, because failure springs from wrong principles, which need to be identified and changed before the pendulum can swing to success.

Those individuals and groups that have a pattern of happiness and success should know that there are some true principles involved, which need to be identified and strengthened.

Some final examples:

1. One Who Has Taken Control

Dennis Wholey, author of *Are You Happy?*, as quoted in *Parade* magazine:

> I was miserable. My life wasn't working, personally or professionally. After 20 years of therapy, I was afraid I was never going to be happy.
>
> In the most important meeting of my life, I talked with Father Vaughan Quinn, director of the Sacred Heart Rehabilitation Center in Detroit. For three hours, I poured out my life's story of anger, loneliness, hopelessness and thoughts of suicide. Father Quinn listened to it all without interruption. When it was his turn, he said it simply: "The problem in your life is alcohol."

There it was: a single principle, extracted from an overall pattern. It had ruled his life and predicted his future.

Wholey continues:

> He was right.
>
> My father was an alcoholic. Like millions of others raised in any kind of dysfunctional home, I wrongly believed as a child and later as an adult that I was not someone who deserved to be, or could be, happy. I handled my frustrations and disappointments with liquor and Valium.
>
> I looked to other people to make me happy and sought their approval and love through my accomplishments and success. . . . When a job ended, as jobs always do, or when people moved out of my life for their own reason, I would isolate and drink.

By conquering alcohol, he changed the principles in his life and broke the pattern. In the article he concludes:

> The happiness we are looking for, I've learned, is already inside of us. Our mission is to discover our own individuality, uniqueness and goodness and to affirm the goodness and wonder of other people. We must love each other unconditionally, without thinking: 'What's in it for me?' We must love others for their own good and not ours. If we do good things for others unselfishly, they will love us in return, which will make us feel wonderful about ourselves—and that's happiness.

Questions for you, from "One Who Has Taken Control"

- *Do you know anyone else who has "turned his life around" as a result of similar insight?*

- *Have you ever rejected a suggestion from a friend or counselor on the grounds that it was an oversimplification? Was it?*

- *From Wholey's description of the principle that he is using to replace alcohol as the solution to his problems is accurate, can you predict his behavior if he should lose his job now? If a friend should move away?*

2. One Who Has Lost Control

A college professor I'll call Siegfried discovered some concepts in his years of research and teaching which enabled him to start a small consulting business that was soon successful. Originally he ran all aspects of the company himself, but it soon grew too big for that. He took on employees and taught them his methods, which he insisted that they apply in a very precise way.

Now, Siegfried had never been in business before; he had spent his whole life in the classroom, where his word was law. Perhaps because of that experience, he had a "monopoly mentality," a conviction that he had a corner on knowledge and need not listen to anyone else. As his business grew, the financial rewards he was reaping reinforced his conviction that *he was uniquely qualified, the sole source of wisdom*. He treated his employees as if they were all first-semester freshmen.

> The financial rewards reinforced his conviction that he was uniquely qualified, the sole source of wisdom.

Whenever a suggestion for change in the product was made, he brushed it aside. When someone pointed out what the competition was doing, he snorted in derision. Any employee who tried a different tack in marketing was severely chastised.

As long as the company remained relatively small his methods worked, because he *was* a competent individual. As he became more and more dependent on the efforts of his employees, however, the consequences of the principle on his belief window began to show up. Able employees who had helped his growth began to leave, unable to find career fulfillment in an atmosphere that was more patronizing than partnership. Customers who made requests for special assistance began to go elsewhere, turned off by Siegfried's insistence that they "take it or leave it" (after all, *he* was the authority on what they needed, not they). Competitors began to take away large chunks of his business, but still he would not change.

Although his "monopoly mentality" had worked for him in one context—the classroom, where he was known as an excellent (if somewhat autocratic) teacher—it failed him when he tried to transplant it into the world of business.

> ### Questions for you, from "One Who Has Lost Control"
>
> - *Have you ever experienced success for a time and then, while still doing things the same way, watched it turn to failure? Looking back on it, can you find a point at which you should have changed your methods, but were too stubborn to do so?*
>
> - *Even if the current sales figures were high, would you be willing to buy stock in Siegfried's company?*

3. One Who Correctly Read a Pattern

You're probably familiar with the story of Mohandas K. Gandhi, the father of the modern India. He knew what he wanted—independence for India—and he adopted the principle of nonviolent confrontation to get it. Holding no office and owning little more than the homespun cloth he wore, he confronted the strongest military power of his time—indeed, the largest geographical empire the world has ever known—and brought it to its knees, depriving it of its largest colonial possession. He bested Winston Churchill, who had said, "I did not become the King's First Minister to preside over the liquidation of the British Empire."

But let me tell you another story, from an acquaintance who served in the U.S. Army at the time of the Allied occupation of Germany after World War II. The city of Berlin was under joint control of the Americans, British, French, and Russians, and officers of these four powers would often meet and work together. On one such occasion, a Russian soldier was accused of a serious crime, and a court of inquiry was called to investigate.

The Western officers followed careful legal procedures while questioning the man, and the Russian officer grew tired of it all. He broke in and demanded, "Did you do it?" The accused, trembling with fear, admitted that he had. The Russian officer then calmly drew his pistol and shot the man. He had the right, he told his astonished colleagues, of summary court martial, given him under Russian military law. The man had been guilty, and was now properly punished—case closed.

Now, with that image in your mind, go back to Gandhi. We would say that the principle he adopted was a correct one, because it worked—it got him what he wanted, in the face of a hugely powerful adversary. But *it worked because it fit with the principles that his adversary had bought.*

Gandhi succeeded because of the British tradition of the Rule of Law and the British principle of Fair Play. Had he appeared before a trigger-happy Russian officer with his nonviolent demands, he would not even be a footnote in history. Gandhi read the pattern of the British courts, the British press, and British politics, and accurately predicted how they would react to him. His success depended not only on following a sound principle himself, but on his ability to read patterns correctly, thus determining (and working with, to his advantage) the principles of his adversaries.

> **Gandhi succeeded because he read the pattern of the British courts, press, and politics, and accurately predicted how they would react to him.**

Questions for you, from "One Who Correctly Read a Pattern"

- *Would it be of benefit to you to know what was on another's window before you started dealing with him or her?*

- *Do you know people who thrive in one culture (corporate or societal) but fail in another?*

The Eccentric Tycoon

People always ask me about Howard Hughes. (No, I never met him.) He was, of course, a highly successful, internationally known businessman. His daring and business vision built billion-dollar corporations and his name is a household word. He ended up, however, in a hideous behavior pattern, moving from place to place as a pitiful recluse, malnourished and in perpetual hiding. That's not as easy to diagnose—what happened?

I can't pretend to give a full answer to that question, but I think I do have an insight. I'll give you some data. Hughes was always eccentric, by normal standards, but he didn't go into hiding until the TWA lawsuit started in the late 1950s. The litigator he hired to represent him in that case, Chester A. Davis, entered his life at that point.

Now Davis, although brilliantly schooled in the law, actually knew little or nothing about business. (If you spent any real time with him discussing business concepts and theories, you would quickly discover that.) But Davis was never shy about expressing his opinion on virtually everything. Thus, a brilliant businessman who is now besieged by the legal system surrounding a major lawsuit starts being advised by a brilliant and aggressive lawyer with huge areas of ignorance about business—a change in the previous pattern. Can you begin to understand and predict what will happen?

Even billionaires are not immune from the effects of having incorrect principles on their belief windows.

From all this I suggest the following: Hughes (who did not have a college degree) bought the principle that Davis, ultimately, could never be challenged on any legal matter. Davis, on the other hand, bought the principle that his legal training gave him the right to speak authoritatively on any subject.

When Davis told Hughes he had to avoid being served by a subpoena, Hughes went into hiding, perhaps against his own inclination, but in deference to the lawyer's advice. Once in hiding, Hughes became far more dependent on his assistants for information than he had ever been before —one of those assistants was, of course, the same Chester Davis, who authoritatively expressed his opinion on everything and whose opinion was often counterproductive. The sum total of these two windows interacting was a pattern of blunders, which continued throughout their lives. You can trace the decline of Hughes's fortunes from the date of Davis's entry into his life, even though Davis performed admirably for Hughes in the courtroom.

Even billionaires are not immune from the effect of false principles on their windows.

In summary:

> **Principles control behavior; if you can read a pattern of past behavior, you can identify the principle at work, and predict the future (including your own).**

It is in the next section that we learn how to turn this predictive power into control.

The Control Model

Everyone knows someone—let's call him John—who learned as a youngster that "practice makes perfect." He applied this principle to every aspect of his life while he was growing up—homework, music lessons, sports, and so on.

John is now out of college and successful in his business. Remembering fondly the experiences he had playing golf while in college, he decides to take up the game in earnest. Because "practice makes perfect," John can be found at the driving range three mornings a week, continually driving balls off the tee into the net.

When John gets out on the golf course, he has a slice that he seems to be unable to correct. John finally decides that the time has come to see a golf pro. Standing before the pro, John demonstrates his driving technique, which the pro videotapes so that he can show John, in visual fashion, where he has gone wrong.

As John and the pro view the videotape together, John sees himself for the first time through eyes other than his own. He recognizes instantly what he's doing wrong. (Remember the audio tape of the drunk in the Japanese police station?) However, correcting it is going to be more difficult than he had thought because, as the pro tells him, "practice doesn't make perfect—it makes permanent." What John has done in his labors has been to reinforce the error, by repeating it over and over again. His only hope of improving is to make a change consistent with the videotape's perceptions rather than his own.

This is the section of the book where you meet the Control Model. One portion of it will already be familiar to you because you looked at it in Section Three. The function of the Control Model is the same as the videotape in the hands of the golf pro: *to provide you with a visual representation of a subliminal process at work;* the subliminal process you go through when you make decisions. Once you have this process before you in visual fashion, you will be able to do what the golf pro does—make adjustments.

Here it is, laid out in blank form.

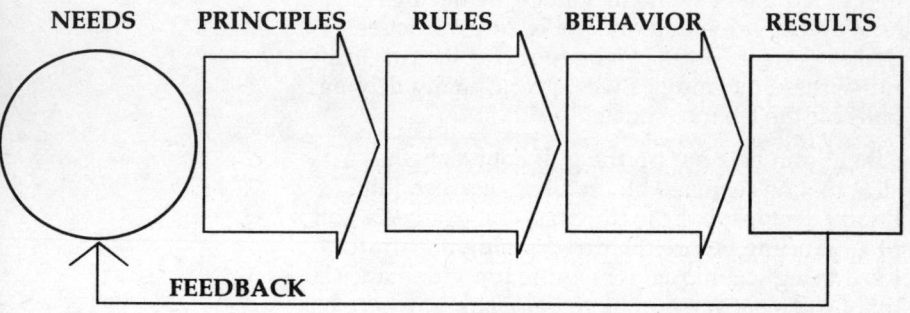

As you can see, the heart of the model consists of the three arrows that we met in the previous section: Principles, Rules, and Behavior. We complete the model by putting a circle in front of

"Principles" and a box after "Behavior"; the circle represents basic Needs and the box represents Results. You read the model from left to right.

Let's go through it, starting with "Needs."

If we wanted to be precisely accurate, we would say that all people really need are the physiological elements—food, oxygen, protection from the elements. However, psychologists have long since discovered that we have psychological wants that are so powerful that they become, in fact, real needs—and the words "needs" and "wants" will therefore be used interchangeably from now on, with respect to this circle.

Basic psychological needs are constantly pushing us; just about everything we undertake is in response to one or more of them. A number of lists have been drawn up to outline what they are, but the one which I will use here comes from a psychiatrist[*] whose views were very popular in the 1950s. He says our basic needs/wants are:

- **We want to live.**

How long? Forever. No one wants to die. Our desire to live is so strong that we will do many things that we would otherwise not even consider, if we feel our lives are in danger. Even when we feel relatively safe, the desire to live manifests itself in our search for a stable job, good health, or even sound investments. For the inexperienced traveler, anxiety arising from the desire to live can be calmed by something so mundane as a confirmed reservation on an airplane leaving from a strange airport. We want safety and comfort and security, all as manifestations of our basic desire to live.

---

[*] whose name, I am sorry to report, I cannot locate. (I made careful notes of his speech when I heard it, and I am sure of the accuracy of the content, but I didn't record his name and therefore cannot give him full credit, for which I apologize.)

- **We want to love and be loved.**

There are few scourges as devastating as loneliness, the sense of being abandoned with no one to love or to be loved by. We go to great lengths to win love. We join groups that don't really interest us because they give us a sense of belonging. We associate with people who do things that are not really in our best interest; we put up with actions that we don't really like; we make incredible sacrifices as husbands and wives and friends, all because of our desire for love, both given and received.

- **We want to feel important (self-esteem).**

"Hey, Daddy, look at me!"

From the very beginning of our lives we want people to notice us and value us. If we cannot win their love, we certainly want to hold their respect. We beam with great enthusiasm when someone discovers one of our accomplishments. We wear fancy clothes that decorate us far more than is needed to keep us warm, drive cars bigger than we need for transportation, and live in houses more ostentatious than we need for shelter, all in an effort to say to the world, "Hey, look at me!"

- **We want variety.**

No one wants to be bored. People climb mountains, take African safaris, try new hobbies, read new books, go to concerts, or take in ball games, "just to break the routine." We want variety in our lives, and sometimes jeopardize (or at least minimize) the other three basic wants in an effort to achieve it. Life, Love, Self-Esteem, and Variety—these are the things show up in our Needs circles. These are basic and they apply to everyone, so we put them in the model:

NEEDS

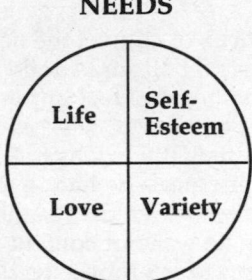

These four are depicted in a circle because, when all of them are being met, our lives can move forward smoothly, like a wheel rolling down the road. However, it is seldom the case that all four of them are satisfied. When a basic need demands attention, the wheel goes flat, and stops:

NEEDS

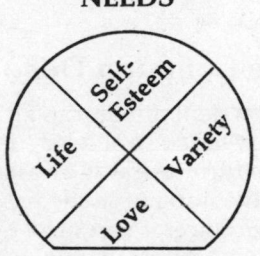

When this happens we begin to channel all of our available resources into the area that is flat in an effort to round it out again. A mother who is concerned about a sick child, for instance, will jeopardize her own health, her need for variety, or the self-esteem she feels from her job, to stay at the bedside of her child, night and day, until the crisis is past and her need to give love is no longer threatened.

Nora, depicted in Ibsen's play "The Doll House," jeopardizes a physically comfortable lifestyle that meets her need in one area in an effort to gain what she is missing in another—self-esteem. The biblical shepherd leaves the "ninety and nine" in search of what is lost.

For the pathological, of course, the need is never filled—the pit has no bottom. Adolf Hitler's desire for self-esteem, his need to feel important with its attendant hunger for power, was so great that nothing would satisfy it. He was not content to be the dictator of Germany—he had to acquire new territory from Czechoslovakia, Poland, Austria, and France. Then he was not content with these conquests—he had to attempt to be the master of Russia, Britain, and eventually the United States as well. Finally, he was not satisfied with the removal of the hated Jew from any position of responsibility in Germany; he sought to destroy the "race" altogether.

As William Borroughs, author of *Naked Lunch* and the "father" of the Beat Generation, has written, "The face of 'evil' is always the face of total need."

Control Is the Common Denominator

There is a common denominator to all four basic needs—control. It was control over such trivial things as how the furniture was arranged in their rooms that gave the nursing home patients their sense of self-importance. It is control over your finances that convinces you that your life is not endangered. Control over your schedule gives you time to pursue a hobby or to have new experiences. Control even surfaces in your need to give and receive love.

NEEDS

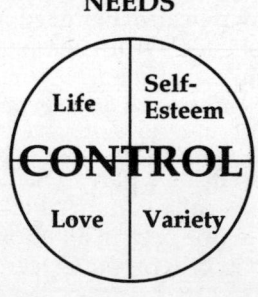

I once spoke with some parents who were having serious problems with their daughter (whom I shall call Angela), whose life was "out of control." She was failing school and showed no concern about it. She had no real friends. She didn't fit in well at home, either, fighting with her brothers and sisters all the time. She had a serious temper, had threatened to run away from home, and, during an argument, had advanced on her mother with a fire poker in her hand. She had been caught with drugs in her possession and openly stated that she had no desire to quit using them. The parents were thinking of putting her in a private school situation where she would "have to grow up." They asked for my advice.

I don't pretend to be competent to handle such therapy situations, but I was deep in the process of working on this book at the time. I looked at the four areas of need in Angela's life—live, love and be loved, feel important, and have variety—and realized that she felt she did not have any control over any one of them. She believed she had no say about what happened at school, at home, in the neighborhood, or at church. She felt unloved, unimportant, and trapped in routine. The only thing she could control, ultimately, was whether she lived or died—and her mother told me that the girl had talked of suicide. Teenage suicide, which is on the rise in America, is, I believe, an adolescent's final attempt to show that there is at least something he can do on his own. So I tried to think of something over which she could exercise control, so that she could begin to feel that at least a few of her needs might be met. I got an idea.

"Why not buy her a pet?" I suggested. "Perhaps a puppy."

My reasoning was this—a puppy gives unconditional love, which she needed, and the relationship between puppy and girl was one in which Angela could feel in control. It would be a start.

"We did buy her a pet," said the father. "A parrot. It bit her."

Somehow that summarized her whole life—even her pets bit her. She turned to drugs.

I wish that I could report that Angela's problems have been solved. Her parents have refused to recognize her drug dependency and take steps to deal with it, so Angela is still in some trouble. Things have gotten a little better, however, as church leaders, working with her parents, have tried to boost Angela's sense of acceptance into a group, thus making her feel more loved and a little more important. Her school work has improved a little as her parents have backed off from pressuring her about it quite so much. Angela feels somewhat less controlled from the outside, and at least is no longer talking about suicide.

So, it is our needs—one of the basic four, or their common denominator, control—that drive us. But where? The "needs wheel" has no direction; it can roll wherever it will (which is why it is represented by a circle in the model). Direction comes from the principles that we buy, which are depicted in the form of an arrow.

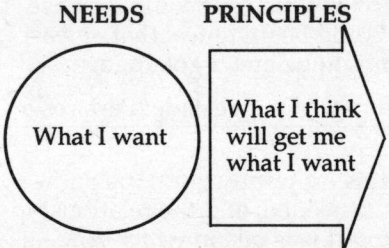

NEEDS   **PRINCIPLES**

What I want

What I think will get me what I want

Think of your needs as the engine in your car; your list of principles is the steering mechanism, determining where your needs will take you.

We walked through the rules and the actions that follow from your principles in the previous section, so I will not review them here. Move past them for now to the last block—Results. It is depicted in the model as a square because it has no movement; in it you list, coldly and analytically, what happened as a result of the things you did.

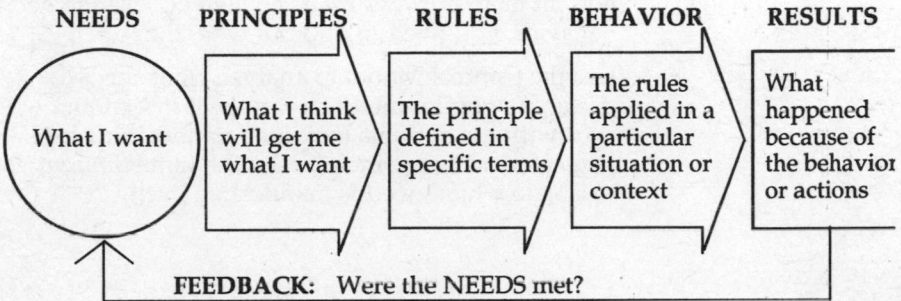

Notice that we've drawn an arrow from the "Results" square back to the "Needs" wheel, to symbolize the act of monitoring whether or not the results met the needs you sought to fill. If the results of your actions do not meet your needs, the principle you are following is most likely incorrect. This is the final "closing of the loop" that should bring you to the understanding that can give you control.

Using the Control Model

The illustration that follows is very simple—indeed, it has been deliberately oversimplified to show how the Control Model works.

Here's the situation: You have a female friend who is "sleeping around" with a wide variety of sexual partners, inviting serious health problems and undermining the possibility of ever achieving a lasting relationship. Her friends believe that she is out of control in this area, and have urged you to do something that will help change her behavior.

If you approach this assignment with a quiver full of facts about risks of pregnancy, dangers of abortion, studies on suicides and depression stemming from unstable relationships, statistics on AIDS and venereal diseases, moral "ought-to's" and "should-have's," you will probably get no-where. Your friend is responding to a basic need and following a set of principles that she has bought in an effort to fill it. To help her change her behavior, you need to find out what they are.

Use the Control Model to analyze what she is doing. As you learned to do in the last section, start with her actions, look for a pattern, and see if you can read her principles. At the same time, try to isolate which need is manifesting itself.

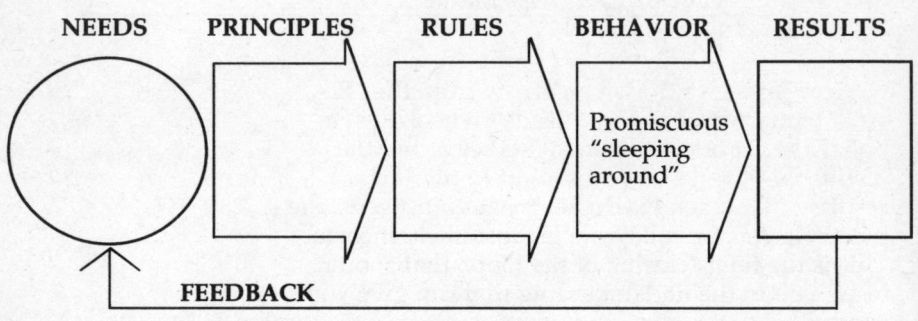

NEEDS PRINCIPLES RULES BEHAVIOR RESULTS

Promiscuous "sleeping around"

FEEDBACK

I'll shortcut this one; for the sake of the illustration, assume from her actions that she is seeking love. The principle she has bought appears to be the idea that "Commitment in a dating relationship comes from being intimate." Plug that into the Control Model, and the rules quickly fall into place, like this:

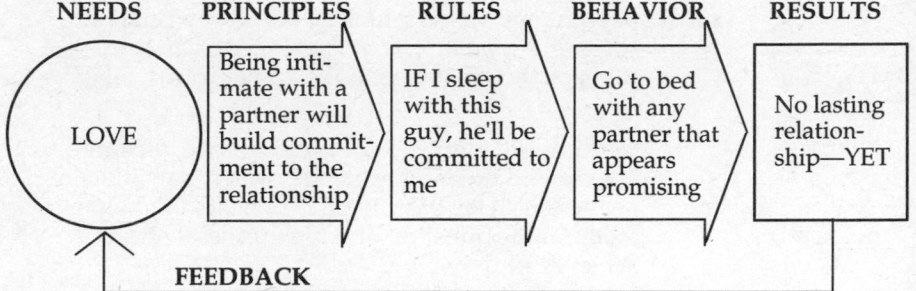

What are the results? Has she found genuine love, or just a series of fleeting encounters? That's the key test of her principle. When you ask the question, what is her answer likely to be?

"Not Yet"

"Not yet" is the answer we usually give when the results are bad, but we aren't prepared to abandon the principle.

If you just point out to your friend that so far she has not found lasting love for her efforts, she will say that the right person just hasn't come along yet—the principle she accepts tells her that. She'll keep kissing frogs in hopes of finding the prince who will commit himself to her. However, if you can get her to consider her results *not* in the light of her *principle* but rather in view of her basic *need*, she might be willing, perhaps for the first time, to confront the question of whether or not her principle is correct. If she does this, and changes principles, then she'll change her behavior on her own.

The key to changing principles is simply the process of examining the alternatives. (Remember, once we buy a principle, it doesn't occur to us that there *are* alternatives.) So, place your friend's present principle next to an opposing one, and ask her to decide which one is more correct. In this case, show your friend a principle identified by psychologists as essential in building a relationship: *True commitment and intimacy requires trust*, perhaps the most essential element in any relationship.

Concentrate your persuasive powers on selling your friend the new principle rather than attacking her actions. Her basic need is to be loved; help her focus on the question of which principle best achieves it.

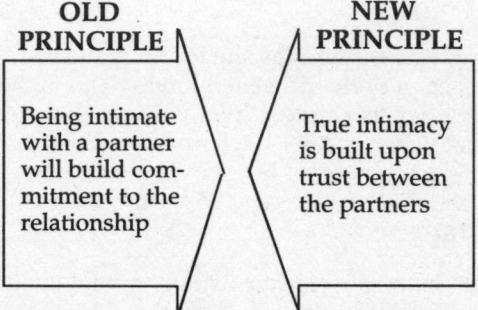

OLD PRINCIPLE

Being intimate with a partner will build commitment to the relationship

NEW PRINCIPLE

True intimacy is built upon trust between the partners

If she buys the new principle, everything else will fall into line. She'll set up some new "if/then" rules and her behavior will change almost without effort.

Why is this so? Psychologists tell us that the mind automatically seeks to resolve the "cognitive dissonance," or inner conflict that occurs when two opposing beliefs or principles try to exist in the mind at the same time. A choice between the principles must be made to restore inner harmony, and clearly seeing the choices helps a person make the right one. If you were successful in making her see alternatives, your friend's new model would look like this:

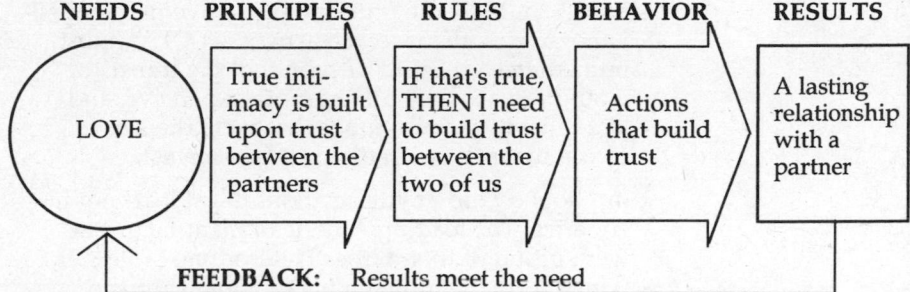

NEEDS	PRINCIPLES	RULES	BEHAVIOR	RESULTS
LOVE	True intimacy is built upon trust between the partners	IF that's true, THEN I need to build trust between the two of us	Actions that build trust	A lasting relationship with a partner

FEEDBACK: Results meet the need

When her results begin to meet her needs, that is proof positive that a correct principle is at work.

The Control Model in Business

The basic human needs have their counterparts in the business world:

- Businesses also want to live, or *Survive*, in business terms. There is a compelling need to make a profit.

- Love is not exactly a business need, but a close cousin, *Respect*, is. Without it, a firm will lose key employees as well as customers.

- A business counterpart to the human need to feel important is the desire most business people have for a sense of contribution, a conviction that their product or service meets a genuine demand. This is closely related to the concept of *Market Niche*.

- Finally, it may well be that *Innovation*—the constant tinkering with product or strategy—is the business counterpart of the human need for variety. It is not just a search for new markets that drives the Research and Development effort in most firms.

"We are free up to the point of choice; then the choice controls the chooser."

—Mary Crowley

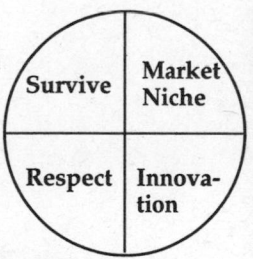

Survive	Market Niche
Respect	Innovation

The four basic human needs have their counterparts in business.

Let's run a business example though the Control Model. In 1947, the transistor was invented by Bell Laboratories, the research arm of AT&T. Almost immediately, it could be seen that the transistor would replace the bulkier, more expensive, and less reliable vacuum tubes that were the key components in any radio or television set.

But nobody did anything about it—at least not in America. The leading American manufacturers were proud of their Super Heterodyne radio sets, which were the ultimate in craftsmanship and quality. These manufacturers announced that, while they were looking at the transistor, it would not be "ready" until "sometime around 1970." The view through their windows told them not to be in a hurry.

Sony was practically unknown outside of Japan at that time, and was not even involved in consumer electronics. But Sony's president, Akio Morita, saw the potential of the transistor and quietly bought a license from Bell Laboratories to use the transistor, for the ridiculous sum of $25,000. (Perhaps there was another concept etched into the windows of the Americans: "Our customers won't buy cheap Japanese products." For those whose window told them that, Sony's purchase was clearly not seen as a threat.)

Within two years, Sony produced the first portable transistor radio, an inexpensive model that weighed only one-fifth as much as a comparable vacuum tube radio. With prices that were only one-third that of a vacuum tube radio, Sony captured the entire United States market for inexpensive radios by the early 1950s, and within five years the Japanese had captured the world market as well.

Using the Control Model, here are the two approaches, analyzed in parallel.

The American View

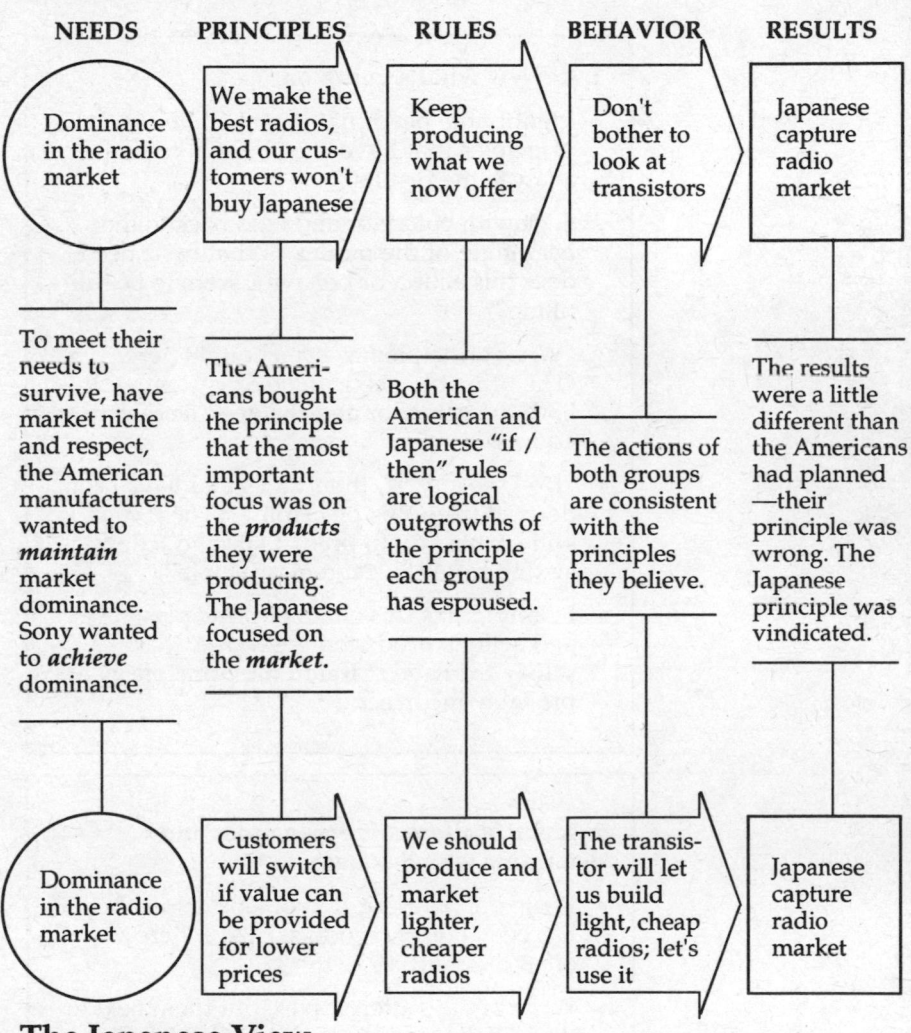

NEEDS · PRINCIPLES · RULES · BEHAVIOR · RESULTS

Dominance in the radio market

We make the best radios, and our customers won't buy Japanese

Keep producing what we now offer

Don't bother to look at transistors

Japanese capture radio market

To meet their needs to survive, have market niche and respect, the American manufacturers wanted to *maintain* market dominance. Sony wanted to *achieve* dominance.

The Americans bought the principle that the most important focus was on the *products* they were producing. The Japanese focused on the *market*.

Both the American and Japanese "if / then" rules are logical outgrowths of the principle each group has espoused.

The actions of both groups are consistent with the principles they believe.

The results were a little different than the Americans had planned —their principle was wrong. The Japanese principle was vindicated.

Dominance in the radio market

Customers will switch if value can be provided for lower prices

We should produce and market lighter, cheaper radios

The transistor will let us build light, cheap radios; let's use it

Japanese capture radio market

The Japanese View

Who achieved control? The people with the correct principles.

Let's go over it again, in summary form, to be sure you understand it.

There are basically three steps:

---

1. Review what's going on.

- Identify the need that must be filled and the principles that have been bought to fill it; analyze the results.

  Start with behavior and read back to the beginning of the model. "What basic need does this action or behavior seem to be fulfilling?"

- "What principle has been bought here?" (The principle needs to be consistent with both the behavior and the need it seeks to address.)

- "Do I see any 'if/then' rules that have been derived from this principle?" (These rules will enable you to predict specific actions arising from the general principle.)

- Finally, "Has this chain of principles, rules, and actions produced the results that satisfy the need?" If not, the principle is probably incorrect.

---

2. Identify alternative principles and determine which is best.

- Write out a description of a principle that has been bought, and ask: "Are there any other alternatives to this?"

- Write out the alternatives, put them next to the initial principle, and ask, "Which is best?"

- Look at patterns in contexts, to validate one principle or the other. Then, make a choice.

> **3. Project the results of your choice.**
>
> - What side effects would this create?
> - Where will this lead over time—is that where we really want to be?
> - Would this truly meet the need?

The answer to that last question will lead you to control. Let's see how it works.

The Control Model at Work

Changing Jobs

I once met with an executive (let's call him Dick) whose contract at his present job would soon be up. He knew that it would not be renewed; he would have to change jobs whether he wanted to or not. He told me of the options he was considering. "Should I switch career paths? I have been in administrative jobs all my life—maybe now is the time to try sales, when I have to make a change anyway." He liked the idea, and seemed almost to be selling it to me, to get me to agree and validate such a course.

"What do you want?" I asked, then, "Why?" I was searching for which need he was most seeking to fill. I then introduced him to the Control Model, and suggested that we walk through it. We began looking for patterns.

He reviewed his past jobs, and what had worked for him. I told him to concentrate on experiences when he had felt truly fulfilled by his job success (when his basic needs had been met). When we had enough examples to form a pattern, it was

clear—administration was his thing; he truly
enjoyed it, and did it well.

We looked at the options he had been considering.
There was one job that fit his past pattern which he
had pushed aside solely because he was feeling a
need for something new (*variety* rearing its head).
However, when he projected the results of this
"something new" option from the pattern of his
past experiences with commission only compensa-
tion, it was obvious that his feelings of security
(desire to live) would be threatened. He would fill
one need at the expense of another. As we talked it
through, Dick decided to take the administration
job after all, and satisfy his need for variety in
other ways. When this decision was made he was
pleased with himself.

Then he got a somewhat troubled look on his face.
"What about my wife?" he said. "She has needs,
too."

Indeed she has. What are they? What does she
want? We put his wife's needs into the Control
Model.

He quickly saw that if he took the job he had just
decided on, which was in a distant city, she would
have to move away from civic and cultural activities in which she was heavily involved that were,
at present, meeting *her* need to feel important. Dick
told me that his wife had bought the principle that
these activities could be carried on only in the city
where they now lived.

"Is that a correct principle?" I asked. (See how easy
it is to be a counselor? All you do is ask questions.)
Well, he wasn't sure. He didn't think so, but she
did.

"So," I said, "you've either got to get your wife to
buy a new principle or you'll have to look at some
of your own again." He commented, "This is a
great tool for introspection, isn't it?" The next day
Dick called me. He and his wife still had not
decided what they were going to do (he ultimately
took a job in the same city, so it is clear that her

needs played a vital role in their final decision), but he wanted to tell me that he had just finished a session with two employees (let's call one Harry, the other Tom) who had a problem that had been festering for many, many years. It had finally exploded that very morning, because of an unusually stressful circumstance. Both Harry and Tom had shocked Dick by saying that they were seriously thinking of quitting. Dick started drawing circles and arrows and squares. "What do you want?" he asked. "Why?" And they were off.

By the time the interview was over, Dick said, they had determined that the problem, primarily, had been Harry's failure to read Tom's window correctly. Tom had asked for Harry's help when he first came on board years ago, and Harry had given it. It made Harry feel important, so he kept on giving it—ever since. Tom kept quiet, to keep peace, but he had finally lashed out at Harry—he wanted to do things on his own and Harry's actions were frustrating his desire for control. Harry's window told him he was being helpful; Tom's window told him he was being patronized.

I can't promise that it will always work this way, but Harry and Tom both had an "aha" experience in Dick's office; by identifying which principles needed to be changed, they resolved the problem. Their use of the Control Model had allowed them to concentrate on what was right rather than who was right.

"It works!" was Dick's gleeful report.

Dealing with Family

If I may be so bold, it even works with teenagers. They are at an age when they most need support, and often they get none. Many times Mom and Dad, concerned about what they consider borderline behavior, buy the principle that if they tighten the screws just a little tighter, they can control the kid. As they do, he buys the principle that his parents don't understand him and don't really like him. The "if/then" rule that follows, for him, is that it is useless to confide in them, to tell them anything. So the rift gets worse, the attempts at control on the part of the parents get harsher, and the depressing cycle continues. No one's needs are met; the models look like this:

The Parents' View:

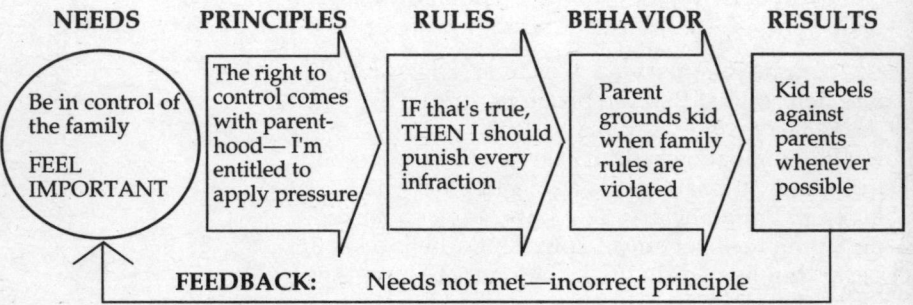

The Teenager's View:

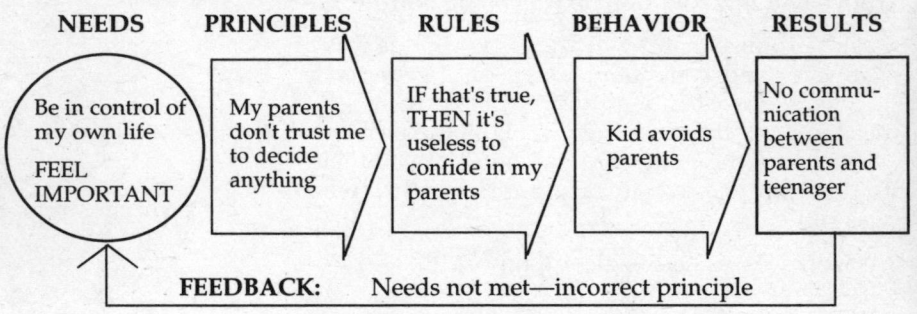

Do these look familiar?

It needn't work that way. One father who understood the Control Model was disturbed about his son's failure to study for a particular class. The usual punishments or sanctions came to mind—no TV until your homework's done, grounded for weekends until your grades come up, etc. Instead, he sat down with his son. What do you want?

The boy was a little suspicious. Dad had never asked him that before. Seriously, son, what do you want? Why? The drill went on until the fact was established that all the boy wanted out of this class was a grade that wouldn't hurt his chances of getting into college. He had no interest in the subject matter, believed it had no bearing whatsoever on his life, and was not concerned in the slightest about the gap in his knowledge that this class could fill. What he wanted was a nondamaging grade. Period.

"Okay," said the father, "that is what you want. How about an A? Would that meet your needs?" Of course. The father filled out the model.

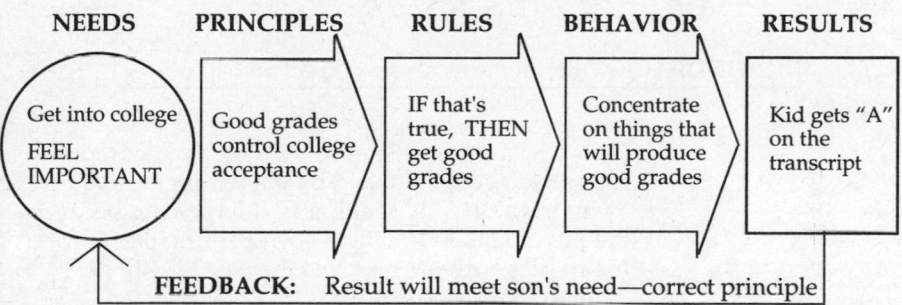

So he mapped out a plan with the boy whereby he could get an A. That was the objective, and that is what they concentrated on. Any learning that took place was purely secondary and incidental; if the boy wanted an A, Dad would help him research what it would take to get it.

"What does this teacher look for? What can we ignore in the course that has no bearing on the grade? What's a special report we can do that will short circuit the tedious stuff? Here's your quickest path to the A, son—go get it."

The boy got his A. He may or may not have learned some of the course material in the process, but he certainly didn't learn any less than he would have if the traditional threats that parents usually use had been applied.

But what did the father want? A better relationship with his son. He bought the principle that the way to get it was by helping the boy get what he wanted, as long as it was honorable. So the father's model looked like this:

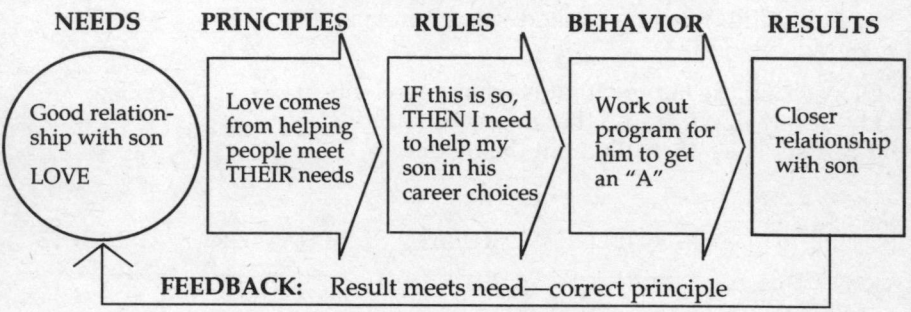

Thus the father's influence over the boy, paradoxically, had been enhanced by his willingness to back away from directly seeking it. It happened because the father was following a correct principle: working to fill another's needs is the best way to get close to that person.

It's Not Always That Simple

Sometimes the principles we follow work in one situation but fail to work in another.

A wife (Rhoda) worked with her husband (Ronald) all during the early struggling years of their marriage. As he went through school and in early entrepreneurial efforts she was heavily involved in his affairs. Being bright and well-educated herself, this was a tremendous help to him. "They are a great team," people would say. "One of the advantages of working with him is that you get her thrown in as part of the deal." Some of their happiest years, as a married couple, were the years of financial struggle. Their model looked like this:

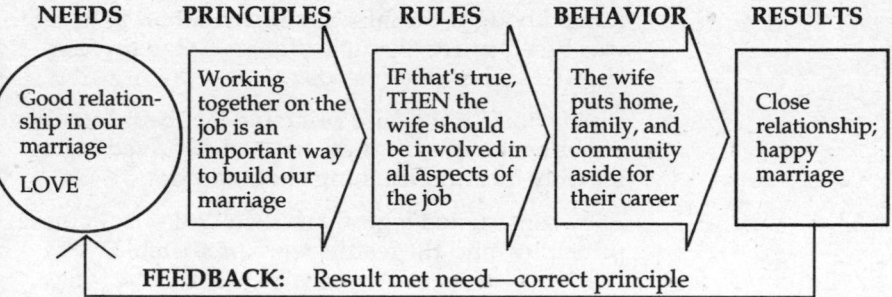

NEEDS	PRINCIPLES	RULES	BEHAVIOR	RESULTS
Good relationship in our marriage LOVE	Working together on the job is an important way to build our marriage	IF that's true, THEN the wife should be involved in all aspects of the job	The wife puts home, family, and community aside for their career	Close relationship; happy marriage

FEEDBACK: Result met need—correct principle

Then the hard work paid off—he joined a large firm that, impressed with his "self starter" pattern of success, posted him to a new office in an Asian country, where executives' wives were not expected to be involved in their husbands' activities except on a social level. As the business boomed, he spent more and more time at the office; she spent more and more time alone. There were no children in the house—they "hadn't had time" because of their working together in the early years. When he became the head of the office, he was away even more. Since it was not considered proper for Rhoda to do anything but sit at home and revel in her new affluence, she became truly bored. Before long, she had a drinking problem, and then there was a divorce.

A native executive of the same firm told me later, "When Ronald was financially able to provide for her every wish and Rhoda stopped working, it seemed to take away all purpose in her life. She believed she was prevented by our culture from doing anything she considered worthwhile. She just seemed to vegetate. I have seen it happen to many wives who come here from America." Looking at it with the perspective of the Control Model, we may say, "They had a true principle, but they were prevented from applying it, so that's why the marriage failed."

That is only partially right; there were some false principles, hidden in the "true" one, which the new context brought to light.

Ronald bought the false principle that his marriage was based primarily on its financial stability; he ignored all her other needs.

Rhoda bought the false principle that being cut out of her husband's business life had deprived her of the only meaningful thing she could do.

They constructed logical "if/then" rules from these principles, and the results were predictable.

Husband's View:

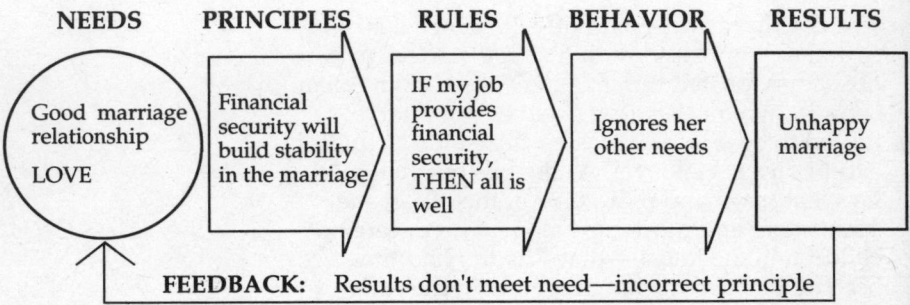

Wife's View:

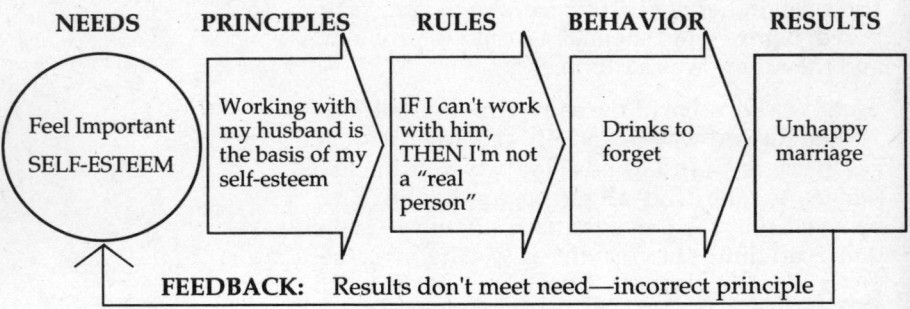

And the marriage failed.

Suppose Ronald had said to himself, "Her sense of self-importance is just as important to our marriage as money"—a new principle for him. It would have led him to ask, "How can I help her maintain her self-esteem now that she can't come to the office anymore?" and his actions would have been different.

Suppose she had said to herself, "Well, I am faced with a new situation, but I am in control of how I will react," a statement of the truth we met in the "Belief Window" section. That would have led her to say, "I don't need the old supports, nice as they were; I will find new ones," and drink would not have been so attractive to her.

Things could have been different. But his belief window and her belief window both conveyed perceptions that needed to be revised to meet the new context. Using the model is not a one-time thing, because contexts can change.

You do not have to move to another country to have marital misunderstandings.

"I can't understand you. What's your problem?"

"I've told you a thousand times!"

Why does one spouse not understand the other's "problem," even after a "thousand times"? Because neither has ever made the effort to see the world through the other's belief window or discover the other's basic needs.

This is what often happens:

In a "traditional" arrangement, where he is the breadwinner and she stays at home:

He says, "Don't I pay for everything around here? Can't you see the need to economize? Can't you even try? What's your problem?"

He doesn't really want an answer to that question; the questions he has asked have already given him his answer—she has no problem.

She says, "Don't you have any consideration for other people? Couldn't that project at work have waited; would the world have come to an end if you had come home on time? Don't you know how much I've slaved over dinner? What is your problem?"

She has a need to be loved, and feels she's losing him to his job; he has a need to be more secure financially (which is connected to his need to live) and feels she's part of the problem.

Each needs to see the other's basic need and be sensitive to it.

In a "modern" relationship:

She says, "Why can't you give up your male macho complex, and deal with me on equal terms? Do you always have to be on such a power trip? Can't you stand to have a woman earn a living? What's your problem?"

He says, "Whatever happened to femininity and spontaneity? Why can't you stop insisting on commitments? What's your problem?"

Each of them is striving for control, to meet his or her own need, rather than to help the other.

In a *good* relationship—modern, traditional, or otherwise:

He says, "What does she want? How can I help her get it? What principle am I following here? Is it correct?

"How does my belief window differ from hers, and how can we best explain to each other what we are each trying to get?"

And *she* says the same, changing only the gender of the pronouns.

As I said,

> **The Control Model focuses not on *who* is right but on *what* is right, because it recognizes that, at base, we all want the same things.**

In the Business World—Dealing with Customers

The following is from *FORD, The Men and the Machine*, by Robert Lacey:

Edward S. Jordan, founder of the Jordan Motor Car Company, was travelling to San Francisco in his private railcar in the summer of 1923, when the tedium of the Wyoming plains was broken by the sight of a beautiful horsewoman galloping fast towards him. Tanned and athletic, the mysterious rider brought her horse racing up to the railcar to canter alongside Jordan's window for a brief, entrancing moment, and as she wheeled to ride away, Jordan turned to ask a travelling companion where they were.

"Oh," came the answer, with a yawn, "somewhere west of Laramie"—and with that answer, a new way of selling cars took flight. Jordan, a squat, flamboyant entrepreneur with a weakness for white spats and gaudy ties, had been trying to off-load his latest model, the Playboy, onto the American public for some months without success. But now, within minutes, the new advertisement was composed, and it appeared a few days later in the "Saturday Evening Post":

Somewhere west of Laramie there's a bronco-busting, steer-roping girl who knows what I'm talking about . . . the Playboy was built for her.

Built for the lass whose face is brown with the sun when the day is done of revel and romp and race . . .

There's a savor of links about that car--of laughter, and lilt and light—a hint of old loves—and saddle and quirt . . .

Step into the Playboy when the hour grows dull . . .

Then start for the land of real living with the spirit of the lass who rides, lean and rangy, into the red horizon of a Wyoming twilight . . .

The Playboy was a rotten car. But the fantasy that Edward Jordan wreathed around it—great outdoors escapism laced with the promise of some muscular sex--extended its showroom existence magically past its natural life, and motorcar advertising was never quite the same again. Edward Jordan's copy told the would-be car purchaser nothing about the horsepower, cylinder capacity, or power-to-weight ratio of the Playboy. It was not even possible to discover from the advertisement how many seats the car had, or how many wheels. But that was not the point. "Somewhere West of Laramie" sold excitement.

What does the customer want? The same things in the "needs wheel" that we all want—to live, love and be loved, feel important, and find variety. Businesses that ignore these wants in either their products or their advertising will soon be out of business.

Edward Jordan had, in Lacey's words, "a rotten car." But his ads promised variety and a sense of importance to those who bought it, and some accepted the principle that these results could indeed come from owning one of Jordan's cars. When the true principle of cars—basically, they exist for transportation rather than "excitement"— replaced false images on the customers' windows, Jordan's automobile company ceased to exist. But the process of appealing to customers' basic needs lives on.

Why do people buy Mercedes cars when *Consumer Reports* says that Toyotas, at half the cost, are just as reliable, and deliver you to your destination just as quickly? Perhaps it is because driving a Mercedes makes one feel more important than driving a Toyota does.

The application of the Control Model to customers is simple when you remember that customers are people, too.

Why do people spend so much money on makeup and perfume, fancy haircuts and after-shave? Could it be linked to the desire for love? (The head of a large cosmetic firm says, "We sell hope.")

Does this concept apply to new products? I was once approached by an entrepreneur who was thinking of launching a new company. He asked me to look at both the product and the marketing plan. I introduced him to the Control Model.

"These are people's basic wants or needs," I said. "How does your product meet them?"

As we discussed "positioning" the product in the marketplace, we considered "positioning" it against the customer's basic needs, to see if we could make him or her feel more secure, more loved, more important, or less bored. Together, we found a marketing approach that was geared to customer needs and the principles customers had bought to fill these needs.

The application of the Control Model to customers is simple, when you remember that customers are people, too.

Dealing with Foreign Cultures

One of the things I enjoyed most about my assignment with Microsonics Corporation was the opportunity it gave me to travel to, and do business in, Japan. We originally organized a joint venture with Time, Incorporated, known as Time-Life Microsonics, which was run by officials of Time-Life Books in Tokyo. Later, Microsonics purchased Time's share in the company and renamed it Microsonics Japan, Incorporated. One of the members of the board of this company at the time I joined it was Frank Gibney, who had been the head of Encyclopaedia Britannica's activities in Japan.

Frank moved very easily in both the Japanese and American corporate cultures. A member of the armed forces in the Pacific during the Second World War, he had been involved in interrogating Japanese prisoners and, in the course of his career, had picked up both the language and a Japanese wife. At the same time, he was a respected vice president of the publishing giant that headquartered in Chicago, Illinois.

I found Japan fascinating but baffling, a reaction that I think is fairly typical among Americans who try to do business there. I did my best to absorb all the lessons I could from our Japanese manager, Terry Arimatsu, but my progress was slow.

Then Terry gave me a copy of Frank Gibney's book, *Miracle By Design*. "Read this," she said. "Frank has done a pretty good job of capturing the essence of what Japan is all about."

Since this was before Kurt and Jerry and I started work on the book, I did not have the perspective of the Control Model at the time. However, I've gone back over it again and realize that what Frank has done to make Japan understandable for American business people is to identify not the basic statistics of the Japanese economic resurgence since the Second World War, but the basic principles that are written on their collective window. (David Halberstam has done much the same thing in his book, *The Reckoning*.)

Gibney identifies two of the more powerful principles that the Japanese have bought. The first has to do with the American military occupation after the Second World War. Gibney describes it with more sophistication than this, but it basically boils down to the acceptance of the idea that "if it comes from America, it is bound to be good." (This applies to concepts and techniques, not necessarily individuals.) With that principle firmly on their windows the Japanese, during the period of General MacArthur's reign as viceroy, accepted almost without qualm such completely innovative ideas as women's suffrage, labor unions, abolition of the nobility, and, of course, American concepts of free enterprise and techniques of management. They gave a Japanese twist to some of these concepts, but Gibney points out, as have many other observers, that the heralded "Japanese style of management" actually had its beginnings in America.

The widely heralded "Japanese style of management" actually had its beginnings in America.

The second principle that he cites is the *respect for harmony* that is at the base of Confucian philosophy. On an island as small as theirs, surrounded by a population as large as theirs, Japanese people have accepted the principle that harmony is the basis of an orderly society. (Gibney's observation is that Americans accept *justice* in that role.)

With that in mind, Gibney points out that most Japanese unions—certainly the ones that matter—are what Americans would call "company" unions. While an auto worker at Ford might feel that he has "solidarity" with his counterpart on the assembly line at General Motors, and thus pay into a common strike fund, an auto worker who labors on behalf of Toyota would feel that it would upset the harmony of his union with his company if he were to put the interests of the auto workers at Nissan ahead of those of the management at the Toyota Motor Company.

Once I understood these two principles and figuratively placed them on the windows of the Japanese with whom I dealt, I became much more comfortable doing business in that country. I'm still no expert, by any means, but I at least have the basis of understanding.

The Control Model and Learning and Teaching

Let's turn to the classroom. A teacher who works with problem children struggled for years with the challenges of his job, reading all the psychology books and teaching manuals he could find. Although he was well prepared, in the traditional sense, he felt constant frustration as he saw student after student move through the system without any positive effects being shown. (Understand that he gets the kids of "last resort"—when they come to him, they are one step from being expelled.) He often felt that he was simply warehousing them until they reached legal age to drop out.

After he had been introduced to the Control Model, he decided to try it in the teacher-student relationships that he faced. He started with a girl whose T-shirt proclaimed her window's view of her self-image. It read: "Beyond Bitch."

Gathering her and the others around him, he asked, "What do you want?" He got blank stares.

He persisted. He went through the whole model, circles and arrows and squares. He told them they were really in control of their lives, discussed the image of the puppet and the puppeteer, and asked again, "What do you want?"

Students who were usually sullen and lethargic became interested and alert. "It was the first time I had all these kids with me, mentally," he said later. "It was amazing." It soon became very clear what they wanted—control, the common denominator of the four basic needs. They were turned on by the idea that they could get it. How? By following correct principles.

That sounded a bit preachy, at first. What are correct principles?

Those that meet your needs.

"So," said one, "if taking drugs makes me feel important, or gives me variety (or whatever), I can do it—right?"

"Right," said the teacher, "*if* taking drugs meets your needs. But what if it *doesn't?* Then you will be following a false principle. You will *lose* control."

"How can I know which it will be unless I try it?"

The teacher discussed the concept of seeds and fruits. If the fruit of a tree is bad, it comes from a bad seed; if the fruit is sweet and juicy, it comes from a good seed. You can't tell from the seed alone, but you can check other trees of the same kind that are full grown. Find someone who has been on drugs for long enough to test the fruit and ask him.

They talked about that. Someone mentioned Elvis—he used drugs to get what he wanted. Why? They constructed a model that looked like the one shown on the next page:

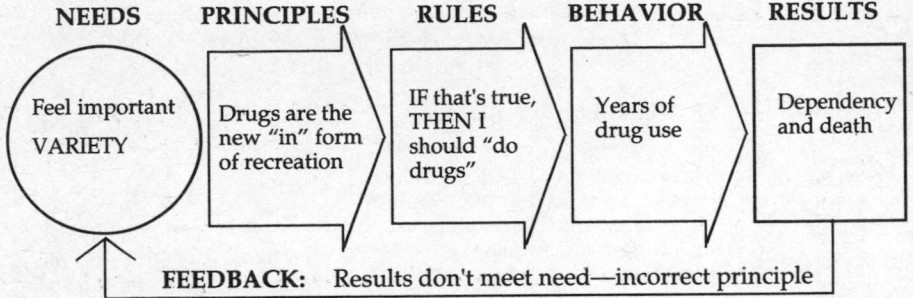

Bad *fruit*, bad *principle*.

Mind you, this was not the teacher "preaching" to the kids—this was the conclusion they came to on their own.

Now, according to the teacher, these students examine everything in the light of the control model, the belief window, and the puppeteer. When someone does something in the group, another will say, "What principle is that?" or, "Come on, untie the strings." New students who join the group are quickly taught both the vocabulary and the concepts (by the students, not the teacher).

He even frames his curriculum in terms of principles and analyzes subjects from that perspective. For the first time in their entire educational experience, he says, these problem students are interested in school, because they believe they are learning something relevant to them—*something that will allow them to control their lives*. The teacher says, "In all my years of teaching, this approach, centered on principles, has produced the best results in the least amount of time."

Dr. William Fox, a college history professor, has taken this concept one step further. The traditional teacher-student relationship says that the teacher must establish and maintain full control over the learning process. It is the teacher's duty, then, to do the research and then tell the student what to learn; it is the student's duty to memorize and repeat back whatever the teacher teaches. Put into the Control Model, the relationship looks like this:

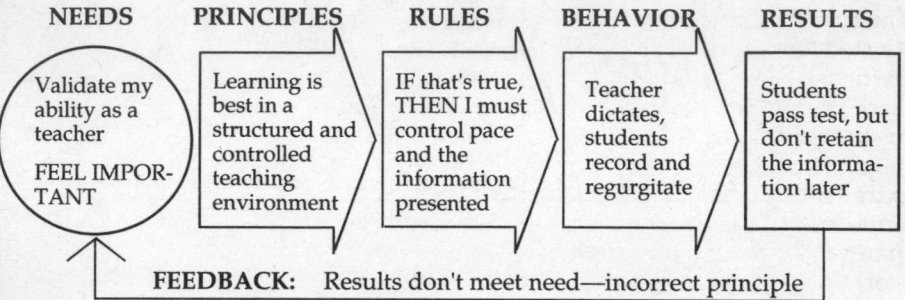

Dr. Fox decided to try turning the process around. What would happen, he wondered, if he adopted the principle that the *student* should be in control of the learning process? Well, it might work like this:

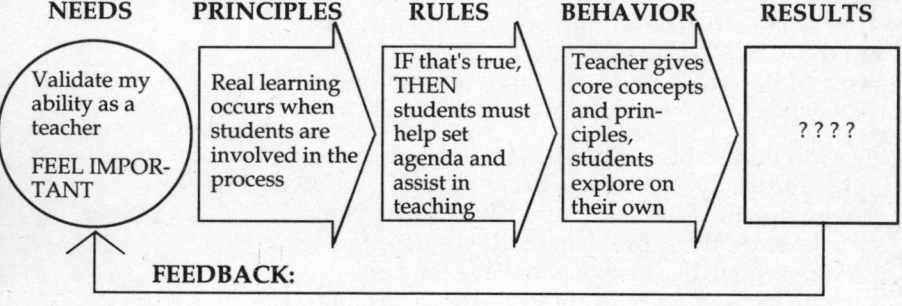

If he took actions to implement the "if/then" rule, would it work? He didn't know, but the scientific method dictated that it was worth a try. He decided to seek to enable his students to take control of the learning procedure as quickly as possible.

How could he do that? He began to experiment a little, and finally found the process that works.

"I do two things with my classes," Dr. Fox says. "I teach them both the *subject* and the *process* of *extracting the principles* of the subject. Of the two, *the extraction process is by far the more important.*"

The results he is achieving are phenomenal. Minority students who previously were unwilling to participate in class discussion now often take the lead. With a class size well above fifty, he has no discipline problems or tutorial requests for special help. Those students who have picked up the extraction process quickly have identified the principles of the subject matter so thoroughly that many of them have completed the entire course work in less than half the allotted time. He allows them to take the final whenever they are ready, and reports a very high percentage of superior grades.

Best of all, the students are "turned on to learning," because the results meet their needs.

"Under the old system," Dr. Fox reports, "the students' only motivation for learning was to be able to give back facts to me on the test. The course had no relevance beyond that. Now, when the students understand the relationship of principles to basic needs—whether those needs are individual or organizational—they realize that they can control their own learning process and use these principles in their lives outside of the classroom. By giving them control over the learning process, I have turned them into colleagues instead of wards. Several of them can teach the subject better than I can."

Of Americans and Kings

I don't teach history, but I do use this example of how the process can work in politics. (I use political examples of the past because they arouse less passion.) Instead of reciting dates, battles, generals, etc., in the American Revolutionary War, I ask the question: What principle was written on King

George III's window, as he viewed his place in the scheme of things?

The answer is the concept of the Divine Right of Kings. He firmly believed that George III was king because God had chosen him to be king, and that the various earls, barons, dukes, and other nobles held their positions by the same principle. God was responsible for their elevation in society.

Given that, what did George think of Americans? Not only had God made them commoners, He had caused them to be born outside of England. As colonials, they were the least noble of all.

What was on the Americans' window on this point? Speaking for them all, Thomas Jefferson wrote, "We hold these truths to be self-evident, that all men are created equal, that they are en-dowed by their Creator with certain unalienable Rights . . ."

King George considered Americans inferior, by act of God. Americans considered themselves equal to the king, *by act of God.* This sets up the basis of the conflict, a framework into which the petitions, decrees, troop movements, and battle orders can be placed. Each side was defending God.

Skip to the Civil War, and apply the same pattern. What did John C. Calhoun and the Southern secessionists believe about slaves? That they were property, so defined in the Constitution, laid down by the Founding Fathers.

What did Abraham Lincoln believe? That all men are created equal, as stated by the Founding Fathers.

It is the same pattern—two sides, both responding to principles springing from the highest authority as they perceived them.

With that in mind, now ask yourself:

Whose dictates were the Jews obeying, when they flocked to the newly founded State of Israel in 1947? And why are the Arabs convinced that they must refuse to recognize Israel's right to exist?

Knowing what principles are at work can help you understand many seemingly "random" or "illogical" things that happen, even when dealing with world problems.

Summary: To make the control model work for you, go down this checklist:

- **What do I want? Why?** (Or, what does the other person want, and why?)

  Which of the basic needs am I seeking to satisfy? Is it in appropriate balance with the others?

- **What principle have I bought to get it for me?**

  How does it compare with its alternatives? Where does it fit in the present context of my life? Has anyone else followed it to success--or failure?

- **If it is false, am I really willing to change it?**

When you can truly go through this list objectively and answer the last question affirmatively, you are on the way to controlling your life.

"The Map Is Not the Territory"

— Alfred Korzybski

Late medieval times were hard ones for the Christian kingdoms of Europe. The Moslems had taken control of the Holy Land and the Crusades were not dislodging them. It seemed that infidels were pressing on every side: Mongols pushing from the east, zealous followers of Islam controlling all of the Holy Land and North Africa, others holding a sizable foothold in Spain. These were bad times for the keepers of what was once the Holy Roman Empire.

The European kings, encompassed by enemies, longed for allies—other Christian kings who had succeeded against the Moslems in their own realms and who might be in a position to attack the infidels from the rear or on their flanks.

It wasn't long before the royal imagination got the better of the kings. After all, there really "should" be such a king elsewhere. Wasn't it a "fact" that St. Thomas carried the message to the fabled Indies? Surely something must have come of that.

Exactly how the rumors got started is lost in history. But by the twelfth century someone's imagination had created such a king: Presbyter, or Prester, John, a powerful and righteous priest-king who ruled a Christian kingdom somewhere in the unknown lands of the east. Grasping for every shred of evidence that Prester John was real, kings and pontiffs eagerly pointed to a "letter" from the distant king that appeared in western Europe around 1165—"proof" that Prester John not only existed but was eager to join forces with the western kings to liberate the Holy Sepulcher. Medieval mapmakers started locating Prester John's kingdom, placing it somewhere on the unexplored fringes of their charts.

What is amazing is the durability of Prester John and his kingdom in the centuries that followed—even in the face of increasing evidence that the story was a myth. (No one seemed to ask how a mortal could have lived and ruled for centuries.) When Marco Polo and others opened contact with China and India, the whereabouts of Prester John was a subject of intense interest and inquiry. When confronted with strangers inquiring about someone who sounded like a threat to their rule, oriental potentates were quick to suggest that the newcomers look somewhere—anywhere—else, which further indicated that Prester John could eventually be found, but in some other place.

By the early 1400s, Europeans knew enough about the country eastward to finally realize that no Prester John had ever been there. But he had to be somewhere, didn't he? Maybe his kingdom was in Africa. The mapmakers moved the location of Prester John to the dark continent.

The dawning age of exploration was fueled in part by the desire to find him. Prince Henry the Navigator of Portugal had his sea captains looking for contact with the elusive king as they moved down the west coast of Africa, before eventually sailing on to India. Even as late as 1573, the best Dutch maps of the world showed Prester John's kingdom in what is now Ethiopia. The long-lived priest-king who "should have been" died hard.

> "The great obstacle to discovering the shape of the earth, the continents, and the ocean was not ignorance, but the illusion of knowledge. Imagination drew in bold strokes, instantly serving hopes and fears, while knowledge advanced by slow increments and contradictory witness."
>
> —Daniel J. Boorstin

No matter how hard we try to gather all of the facts of a situation before making decisions, we are always faced with a certain number of "unknowns." Since using the Control Model as a decision-making tool, I have had the experience of constructing a seemingly perfect path, either personal or in business, only to see it fall apart in the light of new information. I have "read principles" incorrectly, not because there was anything wrong with the process but because the actions on which I was basing my analysis were an incomplete and unrepresentative pattern of the circumstance involved. I made the most informed decision that I could, but I was tripped up by gaps in my knowledge.

Have you ever constructed a seemingly perfect path, only to see it fall apart as new information became available?

Each of us is confronted with similar situations. We wish we had the time or ability to get the complete picture in front of us before we had to decide what to do, but circumstances simply will not permit that. We have to take the facts we have, fill in the gaps from somewhere, and move ahead.

How do we "fill in the gaps"? Where does the information come from that allows us to complete the picture when only part of it is factually available? The answer should be clear to you by now.

> **We fill the gaps in our knowledge by referring to the list of principles printed on our belief windows.**

There is another word for this process of "filling in the gaps," one that may have some unfortunate connotations for you at first. The word is *prejudice*.

Take prejudice back to its roots and see that it comes from a process of "pre-judging"—making a decision before you have all of the information. While none of us want to consider ourselves prejudiced, the fact is that a process of prejudging is required of every one of us, every day, because we never have all the facts.

The list of principles printed on your belief window is also your list of prejudices.

Put in this context, it becomes clear that the list of principles printed on your window is also your list of prejudices. The girl who thought she was ugly had a prejudiced view of her own appearance. The Harvard MBA who wouldn't trust anyone but himself was prejudiced about people whose educational credentials were less impressive than his own. The NASA engineer who is working on the next shuttle launch has prejudicial views about the mental capacities of members of The Flat Earth Society. The process of prejudging a situation is as natural as breathing; it is our list of principles that we consult as we do it.

That being true, it is important that our list of principles contain as many high moral standards as possible. If, as you look out at the world, you do not see things through any kind of ethical perspective, the prejudicial view that your window gives you will be frightening indeed.

However, just because you need moral principles as well as practical ones on your window, the rules of the Control Model do not change. In both instances you have choices to make, and the amount of control you achieve—how well your needs are met—will always be in direct proportion to how correct those choices are, be they moral or strictly practical. This is because there are natural laws in the universe that operate whether we observe them or not.

The laws of aerodynamics determine whose flying machine will work and whose will collapse on the runway; they apply to all. The laws of nature determine which farm crops will grow and which will wither and die; they make no distinctions between honest and dishonest farmers.

Likewise, the laws of human nature determine who will take control and who will spend his life reacting to others.

Our problem is that we secretly believe that we are immune to natural laws. We try to find the shortcut, thinking we can "beat the system."

Instead of doing the hard work needed to solve a problem, we wave our college degree at it, hoping it will be impressed and solve itself. Instead of learning from someone "lower," we pull our job titles more tightly around us and issue stupid orders. Instead of solving communication problems by listening, we yell a little louder at the other person. We act as if we are immune to the laws of human nature, which is stupid.

We do that not because we are stupid, but because we never really understand those laws properly. All we can understand and react to is our perception of them—our principles, again.

Yes, *the principles you buy are your symbolic interpretations of the natural laws that are at work in your life;* they are like maps of a distant land. If the maps are accurate, they will be useful, but when they are filled with descriptions of the kingdom of Prester John, they will be instrumental in leading you astray.

Too often we secretly believe that we are immune to natural laws. We try to find the shortcut, thinking we can beat the system.

Always remember—the map, no matter how accurate, is never the territory itself.

This talk of natural laws brings to mind an experience I had once when I was called upon to address an audience at a prominent university. I thought my presentation was relatively noncontroversial because I focused it upon what I called the "twin purposes of a university." I identified these as first, discovering truth, through research; and, second, disseminating truth, through teaching. I was rather pleased with myself at the symmetry and alliteration that I had achieved.

However, I set off something of a tempest among certain members of the faculty. How dare I suggest, they said, that there was such an absolute as "truth"? When I postulated that "truth" existed, they insisted, I injected religion into academia, which was simply not acceptable. Only a religious fanatic would believe in such a concept.

I discussed this with my father, who came up with an interesting semantic point.

"All general statements are false," he said, "including this one." In other words, these professors were saying that there is no such thing as absolute truth, and that one can accept that as being absolutely true.

I stand on the position that I took at that university that evening. There *are* natural laws, and they are not subject to challenge. What can and should be challenged, however, are our perceptions of these laws—our principles. As we work with principles in the settings of the Control Model and the belief window, we must always keep in mind that our principles are nothing more than symbolic representations of the natural laws we seek to understand and comply with. The laws won't change, but our perceptions can and should.

> Our principles—even the moral ones—should always be subject to updating as we come to a better understanding of the laws on which they rest.

This means that our principles—even the moral ones—should always be subject to updating and change as we come to a better understanding of the laws on which they rest.

Don't be frightened by that thought; I'm not asking you to cast yourself adrift. Changing principles—even moral principles—does not necessarily mean contradiction or abandonment or compromise. The mathematician changes his understanding of the system of whole numbers as he learns more and more about the subject, but he does not abandon the conviction that two apples added to two apples gives him four apples, learned in the first grade. Change, in this context, means growth.

Apply the concept of "change as growth" to a marriage. Ask a couple that has stayed together for many years about their love, one for the other. It has not been abandoned, but hasn't it changed in texture, flavor, and depth over the years? Most of us who have stayed married have not ceased to love our partners, but we have shed some false principles—even love-oriented ones—as we have moved along the path from first blush of romance to congenial familiarity.

"Yes," you may say, "but I will never change my religious beliefs." Good for you; firmly held religious convictions can be an important anchor in our lives. But if your religious mind-set causes you to stop learning, stop experiencing, stop dealing with others in an open, inquiring way, then it puts you firmly in the camp of religious prejudice, and you will soon lose, in Jesus' phrase, "even that which ye have."

One can stand firmly on moral principles and still grow, and, yes, change in one's understanding of those principles. I know many strongly moral and highly principled twenty-year-olds; I would hate to think that they will learn nothing more about morality in the remaining years of their lives.

What Do You Want?

We have come near the end of the journey on which we have sought the processes in our lives that will bring us control. There is only one more major point still to be made. Before we get to it, however, let's look back at where we have been.

At the beginning of the journey, we outlined several basic axioms, as follows:

- **A feeling of being in control of our lives is so basic to our personalities that it can be described as life-sustaining.**

- **Our lives are the sum result of choices, both consciously and unconsciously made; if we can control the process of choosing, we can take control of our lives.**

As we moved into the book, we met several more, specifically:

- **Our behavior is consistent with the principles we have bought; these principles are written on our "belief windows" and regulate our view of everything in the world.**

- **Our process of "buying" principles comes out of the totality of our experiences.**

- **We adopt principles because we believe they will help us meet the basic human desires to live, love and be loved, feel important, and find variety—to be in control. If these needs are not met in our lives, it is because we are following incorrect principles.**

We then met the Control Model, a visual representation of the decision-making process, designed to provide us with a tool to use in our effort to follow correct principles. After going through many examples of how it works, we came to the last set of concepts:

- **There are natural laws that govern human behavior; our principles are merely symbolic representations of those laws.**

- **"The map is not the territory"—our symbolic representations will never be completely accurate and, if we are going to gain control, we are going to have to face the fact that our principles are in constant need of change and growth.**

With all that before you, there is one last principle for you to learn, to go with the ones summarized above, if you are to gain control. It is this:

> **Your ego is constantly seeking to validate your personal self-worth. The more you seek these validations externally, the less control you will have.**

Each of us has an ego perched on our shoulder, which is constantly peering through our belief window for validations of our worth.

With the ego in control, questions like these come to mind:

- What does this person think of me? Of what I've just said? Of how I look?

- Will those people notice the label on my sport shirt and, if they do, are they well enough informed about fashion to know that only people of taste wear these kinds of shirts?

- (From the "counter culture") Am I shocking enough in my long hair, bare feet, and love beads, or do I need to use foul language as well?

- I haven't had anything to say in this meeting; if I don't speak up, will the boss think I'm not prepared?

These are all ego questions, and there is a common element in them—the answers are under the control of other people. This means that they, and not you, are in control when your ego takes over.

Some Examples

When something good happens—a raise at work, for example—an ego-controlled window will tell you, "You got a raise because you are a good person."

If you get a Rolex watch for Christmas, an ego-controlled window will tell you, "Wearing this watch makes you a better person."

And if something really big happens—say, you win the lottery—an ego-controlled window will tell you, "This proves that you are an exceptional person, one in a million."

This process seems harmless enough, and such good experiences are certainly pleasant when we go through them. But the ego wants to turn them into principles, and etch them firmly into our windows. When things go bad, see what happens if this is done.

Suppose you lose your job. (I know of one man, in the movie industry, whose sense of self-worth was so tied to the validation that came from his job that, when he was fired, he shot himself.) The principles on an ego-controlled window will tell you that this proves you are a person of little worth—"you can't even hold a job." If you accept that, how difficult is it going to be for you to find a new position?

Worse, suppose you are assaulted, or, in the case of a woman, raped? We know from the counselors who deal with these crimes that a common result of such an experience is for the one attacked to feel debased and devalued—it is the victim, often, who is beset with serious problems of self-esteem. (This is particularly true if the attacker is a close friend or relative, as in cases of child abuse and incest.) It happens so often that it is considered a natural reaction.

Natural it may be, but it is not the truth; it is the ego speaking when, if something bad happens to you, you react by blaming yourself.

Set Your Ego Aside

One woman (call her Joan) had that experience, as the rape victim of a very close family friend whom she could not bring herself to accuse publicly. She was introduced to the Control Model in another context. (No one knew of the psychological burden she was carrying.) As Joan gained understanding of the model she shifted the focus of the discussion to the brutal experience she had endured and made this comment. "I see now that he was trying to fill a need in his life, and it was really just an accident that I happened to be at hand at the moment things boiled over for him. He bought an incorrect principle about the way to satisfy his need for love and he took it out on me. I am not responsible for his actions, only for my own reaction to them."

After probing the matter further she said, "This has given me the understanding necessary for me to forgive him, and also myself." She had put her ego to the side, and seen the truth. What he had done was terribly wrong, but she was in no way morally involved.

Again, the principle is this:

> **Your ego is constantly seeking an external validation of your worth, and the more external validation that you think you need, the less control you will have.**

So, as you apply the lessons of the Control Model and look at (not through) the principles written on your window, switch your allegiance from your ego to the truth. Recognize that your intrinsic worth is unrelated to what you own, whom you know, what job title you hold, which lodge or church you belong to, how pretty you are, or what others think of you.

External validations are nice, certainly—who does not feel more important while riding in a roomy, air-conditioned Mercedes than in a stuffy, smelly ten-year-old clunker? But doing it does not make you a nicer person. The only way for you to increase your intrinsic worth is to discover and follow correct principles.

Benjamin Franklin put it well when he said:

"As the happiness or real good of men consists in right action, and right action cannot be produced without right opinion, it behooves, above all things in this world, to take care that our own opinion of things be according to the nature of things."

Questions for You (And Your Ego):

If all this talk about ego and truth seems "magical-mystical" to you (borrowing one of my son's favorite putdowns, used when I get too esoteric in my conversation) try this exercise. For one day, or even one hour, stop after each decision or gut reaction and ask yourself, **"Why am I doing this? What do I want? Is this action based on ego, or truth?"**

Some possible situations:

- You look in your closet and decide that you need some new clothes. Is that the truth, or your ego speaking?

- Someone asks you to join a club and you say you would like to, very much. Are you doing it because of a real desire to further the goals of that group, and to have its members as your friends, or is it because your ego is telling you that membership in that group is something that "good" people have?

- You come back from lunch and are annoyed to find that someone has taken something from your desk. Are you truly inconvenienced by its loss, or is your ego telling you to get mad because someone has attacked you?

- You are considered to be expert at something—sports, music, public speaking, cooking, or whatever—and you hear praise for someone else who does the same thing, and this makes you think less of your own accomplishments. Is this the truth, or just your ego complaining?

- You demand a highly detailed report from a subordinate, insisting that nothing be left out or summarized. Is that because you

> really need the information, or are you trying to demonstrate how important you are?
>
> - Someone says something that offends you. Why does it offend you?

Trying to separate your reactions on the basis of those based on truth and those based on ego is hard—each of us has a real ego, and it is working all the time. However, it is an experience that is essential.

If you are going to gain control, your ultimate allegiance, as you ponder your window and the principles written thereon, must be to the truth.

Know the Truth

The ground has been covered; I have said all I wanted to say. I hope it has been both clear and useful.

However, even if it has been, what I have written cannot give you what you really need to take control, which is the courage to face the consequences, the "aha" feelings that come to you as you confront correct principles for the first time. Many people get a glimpse of correct principles and shy away from them, afraid.

What are people afraid of? Having their needs met? Gaining the inner peace that accompanies the resolution of "cognitive dissonance"? Taking control? These are things to be afraid of?

Yes. Many people feel that these are things to be afraid of because they extract a price. Chaining your ego and following the concepts taught in this book will make you uncomfortable, at least for a while. Some of your most important "aha's" will also be some of your most distressful moments, rather like looking up from the center of the basketball court in an arena filled with fans, and realizing that you are standing there on ice skates, dressed in a hockey uniform.

At least that has been the experience of all of us who have worked on this book. It has not been comfortable for us to understand that we have followed some false principles with single-mindedness, while neglecting obvious solutions that the distortions on our windows wouldn't let us see. That can be embarrassing, like a pratfall on the ice. It is not comfortable to steal a glance through other people's windows at what you have just said to them, or done to them, and realize that you have in fact done and said some pretty stupid things— trying to meet your need to feel important, at their expense.

It is not comfortable for anyone to contemplate his or her real motives, to face the possibility that the "noble causes" espoused may really be just a cover for something less praiseworthy. The ego doesn't like that.

No, it is much more comfortable to curse the world when things do not go right for you, and hope that whatever gods there may be will hear your curse and miraculously set things right (by your standards). It seems more comfortable, often, to live in misery than to exert the effort needed to become happy.

In his play "The Glass Menagerie," Tennessee Williams tells us of Laura, an unhappy young woman whose life was completely under the control of others—the dominating mother, the fictitious "gentleman callers" who never call, the rest of the world who could not, or would not, see any worth in her at all. She coped with all this by playing, like a child, with a set of toy glass animals. It was only with them that she was in control—only there, in the glass menagerie, that she could escape the horrors of the world.

But in the end she did not escape. She was imprisoned in the most dreadful prison of all—herself. By running from the uncomfortable truth, she ended up controlling nothing but a few bits of glass.

Contrast her with the Olympic ice dancing champions, Torvill and Dean, who left the comfort of cozy homes and firesides, ventured out onto the cold and unyielding ice, and found freedom. They have learned the correct principles of body movement and exercise and muscle building. They have learned the correct principles of music and rhythm, and have applied those principles to meet their needs. They have changed and corrected and grown as they have progressed, until finally they have reaped the rewards of control. They are as free in their world as Laura is imprisoned in hers.

When your allegiance shifts from ego to truth, correct principles become more and more clear, and growth is a natural result. When your full allegiance is to the truth—not to your map, not to your prejudices, not to your ego, but to the truth— you can, in fact, take control.

At the University of Chicago, a passage from the New Testament is carved in stone; it is the motto of the school. It is the best counsel we can give, here at the end of our journey:

> **"Know the truth, and the truth shall make you free."**

Isn't that what you want?

Index

Control Model (continued)
    in classroom, 83-87
    in drug-abuse seminar, viii-x
    in family relationships, 71-74, 77-78
    and foreign cultures, 81-83
    in historical scenarios, 87-88
    three steps in using, 68-69, 89
    use of, examples illustrating, 61-63, 66-67,
        69-77
    as visual representation of subliminal
    process, 54
Crowley, Mary, 65

Davis, Chester A., 50-51
Drug abuse:
    education on, vii
    examining, through control model, 84-85
    students involved in, meeting with, viii-x

Edison, Thomas, 32-33
Education:
    Control Model in, 83-87
    principles concerning, 14-15, 50
Ego, 100-105
Eisenhower, Dwight D., 30-31
Evil, pathological need leads to, 58
Experiences, principles emerge from totality of, 32,
    99
External validations of self-worth, 100-105

Failure, false principles lead to, 45
Feedback, 61
Flying machine built on incorrect principles, 25-28
Foreign cultures, understanding, with Control
Model, 81-83
Fox, William, 85-87
Frankl, Viktor, 20
Franklin, Benjamin, 103
Frustrations, 5

Gandhi, Mohandas K., 48-49
Gaps in knowledge, 93
Gibney, Frank, 81-83
"Glass Menagerie," 108

Bibliography and Acknowledgments

Although presented through my voice, the book is truly the collective work of three people—Kurt Hanks, Jerry Pulsipher, and myself; for it we alone are responsible. However, we could not have put it together without the aid of many individuals and publications that have influenced or stimulated our thinking. We gratefully acknowledge the contributions of those with whom we have worked, and those whose works we have read, while absolving them of any of the book's shortcomings.

For the past few years, Kurt Hanks has taught Industrial Design at Brigham Young University, and is the author of several college texts in design. During this experience Kurt has come in contact with a number of faculty members who have made significant contributions to the concepts discussed here. Most prominent among those who have given freely of their time and professional expertise are Dr. John Marshall of the Design Department and Dr. William Fox of the History Department. We are also indebted to many students who have gone through Kurt's courses and have tested many of these concepts in the classroom and in their personal lives.

Jerry Pulsipher approached our collaborative efforts from the background of his own communication planning firm, developing educational materials and programs for many public and private organizations. Working with widely-varying subject matter over the years, Jerry, in cooperation with Kurt, pioneered better ways of identifying, understanding, and communicating the principles that underlie a wide variety of subjects in different disciplines. Jerry acknowledges the contributions of many with whom he has worked, most notably the encouragement of John Rosenow, executive director of the National Arbor Day Foundation.

My own experience in business and government has included contact with a wide range of executives who have taught me the importance of correct principles, perhaps without their realizing it at the time. I feel particularly indebted to James Beggs, former Administrator of NASA (the boss who provided the insights reported in "The MBAs Who Had the Answers), Robert R. Mullen (the young reporter of "The Great Canadian Gray Goose Flying Machine Company"), and William M. Batten, retired chairman of the board of the J.C. Penney Company who, during the five years I was with Penney's, gave me an invaluable background in how a set of general principles controls the organization in which they are applied.

We also acknowledge the contributions of Evelyn P. Metzger, President of E.P.M. Publications in McLean, Virginia, for her willingness to review earlier versions of the book and her insightful comments that made the final version much improved.

Finally, we are indebted to our colleagues at The Franklin Institute, Inc.--Hyrum Smith, Dennis Webb, Richard Winwood, and Lynn Robbins--who have taken these concepts into the corporate world, taught them and experimented with them, and then returned with real life reactions and suggestions. With their help, what started out as theory has been refined into practical and tested advice.

In addition to all of the individuals consulted and listed above, we have drawn upon the following published sources:

- *The Discoverers*, by Daniel J. Boorstin. This is the book that gave us the story of Prester John, and provides a fascinating description of how ideas and perceptions control the flow of history.

- *The March of Folly*, by Barbara W. Tuchman. Starting with the historical account of ancient Troy and moving through the Vietnam War, Tuchman chronicles how a set of beliefs firmly etched into organizational windows can lead to what she calls "woodenheadedness," and result in blind, unreasoning folly on the part of nations and institutions.

- *The Reckoning*, by David W. Halberstam. This is one of those "I wish I had said that" kind of books; Halberstam outlines the principles that were at work in two contrasting companies in the same industry--Ford and Nissan. With those principles clearly understood, he chronicles the predictable decline of Ford and rise of Nissan in the challenge of the post-war automotive marketplace.

- If reading *The Reckoning* does not cause you to overdose on information about the automotive world, read two other books in parallel--*Ford, the Men and the Machine*, by Robert Lacey; and *Iacocca, an Autobiography*. Here is a classic example of how a single set of events looks when viewed through two different belief windows. Lacey's account of Lee Iacocca's firing as president of Ford Motor Company (and the circumstances that led up to it) is very different from the one presented by Iacocca himself.

- *Miracle by Design*, by Frank Gibney. Gibney is one of the recognized authorities on post-war Japan, and here he outlines the differing principles between Japanese and American corporate structures, management methods and cultural philosophy. With these in front of you, you can more accurately predict what a Japanese manager and an American manager might do when confronted with similar problems.

- *Bill W.*, by Robert Thomsen. The story of the founder of Alcoholics Anonymous and the mental processes that he went through as he first embraced, then was dominated by, and finally rejected alcohol as a major factor in his life.

- *Man's Search for Meaning*, by Victor Frankl, and *The Gulag Archipelago*, by Alexander Solzhenitzen. These books are both classics, as they outline the horrors of Nazi and Soviet concentration camps. Each author describes the process through which he went in order to free himself of the dehumanizing experience that his captives had intended to inflict upon him.

- *The Things That Matter Most*, by Lowell Bennion. A small volume in which this noted educator lets us glimpse through his belief window.

- *Innovation and Entrepreneurship*, by Peter Drucker. America's foremost academic commentator on business and its practices takes America's managers to task for their failure to see the basic principles that underlie all business success, and does his best to lay those principles out in cogent fashion.

- *The Marketing Imagination,* by Theodore Levitt. Includes an essay that first appeared in the *Harvard Business Review* on "Marketing Myopia," setting forth a number of basic principles that too many business people have forgotten.

- And, finally, we cannot pass up the writings of Benjamin Franklin, both his *Autobiography,* and a new compilation of his secrets of success, *Benjamin Franklin's The Art of Virtue,* edited by George L. Rogers. Benjamin Franklin has been one of the most productive and insightful individuals produced by America, and the principles that underlay his success are worth reviewing, more than once.